WINNING THROUGH CARING

HANDBOOK ON FRIENDSHIP EVANGELISM

MATTHEW PRINCE

Foreword by
HADDON W. ROBINSON

BAKER BOOK HOU
Grand Rapids, Michigan

Printed in the United States of America

All Scripture references are from the Revised Standard Version of the Bible,
copyrighted 1946, 1952, © 1971, 1973, and are used by permission.

TO JUDY
my wife
and best friend

Foreword

The word *evangelism* stirs up assorted images in our minds. For some timid souls who couldn't sell tickets for seats on the fifty-yard line at a Super Bowl, evangelism conjures up going door-to-door talking to people in strange neighborhoods. For others, evangelism means grabbing people by their lapels to give them a religion that gets no deeper than the shirt pocket. Still others remember courses on "fifty questions non-Christians ask" and the frightening conversation with a non-Christian who brought up question fifty-one. A few of us remember techniques designed to napalm the natives—dropping tracts out of cars and hoping they would find a target.

If that is how you feel about evangelism—and you are not alone—I'm surprised that you have even opened this book. Having had the courage to read these lines, I urge you to read on. Matt Prince presents in the following pages an approach to evangelism that focuses first on what you are, and only then, on what you do. There's more good news.

Out of his study of the Scripture and his knowledge of people he tells us how to make friends before we make converts.

Jesus urged us to do that when he drew a good lesson from a bad example in Luke 16. In that story of an unjust business manager, he told us to use our position and possessions in life to gain friends who would welcome us into heaven. Some friendships are made over trivia—trading baseball cards or collecting comic books. Some friends share common sins. Other friendships focus on common activities—bowling buddies, fraternity brothers or business associates. Certainly all these friendships can enrich your life, yet none will be more satisfying and permanent than friends you introduce to Jesus Christ.

If you know how to make a friend but are not sure you can make a convert, by all means read this book. It may change your lifestyle and your life. But more important, it can change the lives and the eternal destinies of people who live and work with you.

Haddon W. Robinson, **President**
Conservative Baptist Theological Seminary

Preface

Every child of God is a directly commissioned representative of Jesus Christ. Each is everlastingly responsible for the witness he or she does or does not bear.

God lovingly gave His dearest treasure so we could have everlasting life. Many believers literally have poured out their lives so that this message could come to us. Now we have the Savior and we know people who face eternal agony without Christ. Every conscientious Christian sooner or later will come to grips with his great debt. With Paul he realizes that he has an "obligation both to Greeks and to barbarians, both to the wise and to the foolish" (Rom. 1:14).

This is where it seems that many Christians become either frustrated or defeated because of fear or lack of information. Some perhaps delay serious consideration of the issue because of worries, riches, or pleasures.

Yet I am convinced that many Christians genuinely want to see friends come to Christ. They are not content to continue in defeat. This is where I found myself a number of years ago as a busy practicing attorney. The Lord graciously had used many fine people to teach friendship evangelism, but results were lacking. Then, beginning in the mid-sixties, I began to apply the lessons learned from seminary, the Young Life staff, the pastorate, and an active law practice. People began to come to Christ. The effort outgrew the law practice and the New Life Mission began.

One of my deepest longings is to help a child of God reach someone for Christ. What follows are the basic biblical principles of friendship evangelism which grew out of thirty years of Bible study, training, experience, and application. This book is designed specifically to help Christians effectively share Christ in everyday life.

Many vital spiritual prerequisites necessary to maintain proper balance in biblical outreach cannot be fully covered here. For example, Christ should be Lord of every life. A Christian cannot experience God's unhindered power flowing through his life unless the heart has been surrendered to Him. Unless the Lord works our labors are in vain. He must build the house and He only does it through willing hearts.

In addition to one's initial decision of total surrender, he should maintain a strong personal fellowship with Christ in the Word and in prayer. He must live a Spirit-filled life. He should continue in active fellowship with other believers as part of a local assembly.

The brief mention of these essential Christian life truths does not indicate a light regard for them. They are essential to effective witnessing.

This volume is designed to help the willing believer disengage from the holy huddle of believers and go on to embrace those who are outside. Because the effective Christian life begins in fellowship with Christ, learning and appropriating those inward qualities which contribute to making us productive channels of God's power is essential. This volume, therefore, is divided into two parts. Part One deals with the things that must happen on the inside of the believer and Part Two with making things happen on the outside.

Matthew Prince

Contents

PART One

The Inside

The purpose of this book is to help you share Christ with others. Part One shows that things must happen on the inside of the believer before fruit will be seen on the outside. The Christian life begins in fellowship with Christ, where we will learn and appropriate the right inward qualities which contribute to making us effective conduits of God's power.

Chapters 1 through 5 discuss these qualities. We must share Christ's seeking love. A step in the right direction will be taken when we see the dear ones for whom Christ died as victims of the enemy rather than as the enemy. We must cultivate sensitivity to the real issues from God's point of view. Examining our obedience and building our self-confidence can also help us.

1

Why Now?

A rugged mountain man from Tennessee was big-game hunting in Alaska, when he and his guide were charged by a bear. As his guide began firing, the man froze. The guide's rifle ran out of bullets. The bear was still charging, so the guide wrenched the rifle from his guest's hands and continued shooting. As the huge animal dropped a few feet from the men, the mountaineer began to apologize profusely. His guide said, "Don't feel bad. You did just fine." That honest mountain man said, "What do you mean, 'fine'? I froze on you. I was no help at all." The guide responded, "No, you did just fine. Most of the tourists run off with their rifles."

Does the thought of being an effective personal witness for Jesus Christ seem a fearful proposition? Take courage. It begins that way for most of us. If you care enough about Christ and people to have read this far, you're doing just fine. Let me encourage you to continue. You may not have all the answers and you may not have realized much success in touching the lives of others for Christ, but if your attitude is right, God will use you. He delights in guiding those who let Him do so. Trust Him to give you the knowledge and experience you need for each step of this adventure.

Fear Can Be Handled

God is on the throne and has promised to meet all of our needs, so do not let fear immobilize you. Concentrate on God's love for people, and fears will fall into perspective. Be positively motivated by His desires. Begin with the basic question: Why should every child of God get involved in the Great Commission?

For Christ's Honor

Our first goal should be to exalt the Lord. His honor, His worship, His praise are above everything. In order to do this, we need to be in harmony with and obedient to Christ's major purposes. He said that He came to earth to give His life as a ransom for many, to seek and to save the lost. His one Great Commission charges us with the responsibility of taking the Good News to all who are lost in the world's enslaving darkness.

When we are doing Christ's will, other things naturally and supernaturally will fall into place. We will begin to experience self-confidence, power, excitement, and fulfillment, because Christ is the author of life, joy, and fruitfulness. It is basic that everything from excitement to fulfillment will follow if we honor Christ through careful obedience to His Great Commission to the church. A great truth has earned the status of cliché because of its tremendous inherent merit: "When all else fails, read the instructions." Christ's major instructions are clear. Yet ever so imperceptibly throughout church history, God's people have seemed to drift from the first love, the first effulgent preoccupation with His commission. Assorted ailments and apathy inevitably set in. It is never too soon to share Christ's love and to actively set about caring for others. The time is now.

One of the ultimate New Testament truths concerns itself with the theology of now. Now is the only time we have; now is the only acceptable day of salvation (II Cor. 6:2). We may not be here tomorrow. Now is the time to honor Christ by becoming an effective personal witness. Once that decision is made, you can begin to experience a new dimension of God's power flowing through your life. He will give you success.

To Experience the Thrill of Triumph

God has designed us for success. Few experiences in life can match the Christian's thrill of triumph. Paul had what every Christian has the right to possess—confidence that God guarantees victory. He knew that Christ always led him in triumph (II Cor. 2:14). He knew that we overwhelmingly conquer even the most adverse conditions through Him who loves us (Rom. 8:37). More will be said about confidence in Chapter 2. It is enough here to mention that we are born to hope and born to power (Rom. 6:4; Eph. 1:18-20; I Peter 1:3-5). A confident, favorable expectation is part of our birthright as God's children.

But God has called us to more than simply a positive attitude. He has guaranteed success as He defines success. Each

3

Christian is gifted to fruitfulness, not sterility. Christ promises that if we abide in fellowship with Him and His Word abides in us, we will bear fruit, abundant fruit—fruit that glorifies the Father and that lasts forever (John 15:1-16). It must be recognized that fruit cannot be understood to mean only productive personal witnessing. But in light of the Great Commission, fruit cannot be conceived of as excluding winning others to Christ. Christ has commanded all of us to be witnesses for Him.

God has chosen each one of us for a purpose. All have been called to show forth God's praises (I Peter 2:9) and to let His light shine through us in the midst of a dark and perverse world (Phil. 3:11-14). If we are surrendered to God's will, no force of evil can defeat His purpose. We are commissioned to results, not to frustration. When God commissioned us to catch men, to retrieve the lost, and to make disciples, He surely did not intend that we be frustrated in these pursuits (Matt. 28:18-20; Luke 5:4-11; 15:1-10).

The conquest of fear is one of the grandest forms of God's triumph. There is no fear in His perfect love (I John 4:18-19). God has not given us a spirit of fear but of power, of love, and of discipline (II Tim. 1:7). Many people live their lives controlled by fear. We need not cringe in defeat because of fear of failure, fear of pain, or fear of loss. God has promised victory.

Seeing others come to Christ is one of the most singularly rewarding experiences in the Christian life. It gives us a thrill of triumph as great as any other facet of our walk with Christ. A new dimension of enjoyment is injected into our lives.

No one can promise a life of ease. The Christian experience is in part a fierce warfare. Nothing I have said here

is intended to convey the false notion that friendship evangelism will usher you into an exhilarating experience with
no discouragements or letdowns.

Life itself is hard enough without satanic opposition. All
Christians struggle. The difference is that some struggle in
ongoing retreat, adding guilt to apathy. Those who properly join Christ in obedience to His Great Commission
have a great hope even in the midst of struggles, for their
struggles will ultimately consummate in the thrill of
triumph.

To Be Fulfilled

Victory is one thing, fulfillment another. The successful
Christian life is one of balanced growth. Whether a victory
is being experienced momentarily or not, every child of
God can have that great sense of well-being that comes
from knowing that he or she is fulfilling God's purpose for
his or her life.

Christ offers life in all of its fullness right now. God
desires that His children be saturated with a sense of great
well-being (John 10:9-10; 15:11). We can be so full of God's
warmth that His love flows out of our hearts to others
(Rom. 5:5). The Spirit of God dwelling in the heart of every
believer produces this outgoing, God-given life. Christ
described it as rivers of living water flowing from our innermost beings (John 7:38).

Then why are so many Christians frustrated, depressed,
miserable, or unfulfilled? Some are this way because they
fail to maintain fellowship with Christ, others because of
unconfessed sin, some because they harbor bad habits, still
others because of immaturity, and many because of rebel-
lious attitudes.

Yet many Christians are living in fellowship with Christ, confessing known sin. They make a genuine effort at nurtured growth in the Word, prayer, and fellowship with other believers. But still they are unfulfilled. Their lives are sterile. Emptiness characterizes their routine experiences. For all their biblical knowledge, they lack excitement. They no longer expect the vibrant life with Christ. The sparkle is gone or perhaps never was there. Why?

It may well be that they simply have not shared in the main concern of Christ's heart. What can be anticipated in the life of the believer who refuses to become involved in the Great Commission? Guilt in one form or another can be expected in most cases. That guilt frequently is sublimated or buried at the Christian busy board. We look for all kinds of rationalizations to justify our growing self-preoccupation. Then we are in danger of suffering further wounds. Successful Christians constantly seem to appear on the scene, dismissing our excuses for failure. Some insensitively bludgeon us with more guilt. Many of us wind up with an unhappy experience and honestly do not know why. Disengaging from the Great Commission might be the cause.

Christ came to die for mankind. He sought us out. His seeking heart does not have to stop with us. We can enter into a lifestyle that is both enjoyable and fulfilling. Regardless of our gifts or education, we can be the effective witness Christ wants us to be by cultivating the exciting biblical lifestyle that is friendship evangelism.

To Recognize Your Imperative

But this lifestyle is more than exciting; it is compulsory. We must recognize the urgent ultimatum. Those who die without Christ will be in agony forever. Whoever calls on Him will be saved, but many will never know the Savior unless we bring them the Good News. You may be the best representative of Christ that many people know and the only one some know.

We should care. Are we genuinely seeking Christ's desires? Do we know Him better today than yesterday? Are we taking Christ seriously? Will we get down to Christ's main business, or will we continue forever to play at our clannish games, shutting out of our lives those for whom He died?

The issues that face most Christians daily can be illustrated by a Super Bowl scenario.

Every January millions of fans watch what has come to be one of the major sports events in sports-worshiping America: the annual Super Bowl conflict between the greatest of the professional football teams.

The quarterback is one of the classic heroes of this event. His team is behind, 21 to 23. The ball is on our hero's own 25-yard line: seventy-five yards to go. The two-minute warning sounds. The quarterback begins his history-making jog to the coaches on the sidelines. The crowd is tense. The cameras follow him.

Waiting in the huddle for the quarterback's return are ten of the best offensive players in the world. On the other side of the scrimmage line are eleven of the world's best defensive players.

The quarterback jogs back to the huddle. His teammates wait, confident that he brings with him the precise set of plays that will move the ball seventy-five yards in less than two minutes and assure victory.

The camera focuses on the huddle. Seventy-five million sets of eyes wait, unblinking. With ten expectant faces surrounding him, the quarterback looks up and quietly says, "Men, I'm not sure football is what I want to do."

The Christian is in a far more dramatic situation. People lost in darkness, blinded by Satan, are going into eternity. No one has shared Christ with them. They are looking at us, waiting.

To Obey Christ

Christ gave us one Great Commission—to go into the world and make disciples of all the nations. It is stated in one form or another throughout the New Testament.

> And Jesus came up and spoke to them, saying, "All authority has been given to Me in heaven and on earth. Go therefore and make disciples of all the nations, baptizing them in the name of the Father and the Son and the Holy Spirit, teaching them to observe all that I commanded you; and lo, I am with you always, even to the end of the age" (Matt. 28:18-20).
>
> And He said to them, "Go into all the world and preach the gospel to all creation" (Mark 16:15).
>
> And that repentance for forgiveness of sins should be proclaimed in His name to all the nations, beginning from Jerusalem (Luke 24:47).
>
> Jesus therefore said to them again, "Peace be with you; as the Father has sent Me, I also send you." (John 20:21).
>
> But you shall receive power when the Holy Spirit has come upon you; and you shall be My witnesses both in Jerusalem, and in all Judea and Samaria, and even to the remotest part of the earth (Acts 1:8).
>
> How then shall they call upon him in whom they have not believed? and how shall they believe in him whom they have not heard? and how shall they hear without a preach-

er? And how shall they preach, unless they are sent? just as it is written, "How beautiful are the feet of those who bring glad tidings of good things!" (Rom. 10:14-15).

The Great Commission is Christ's purpose for us, His main business, His heartbeat. Anything less than full obedience to it is disobedience. Remember that obedience means fulfilling joy, not unhappiness. If we delight ourselves in the Lord, He will give us the desires of our hearts (Ps. 37:4). Nothing would be more delightful to us and to the Lord than instant obedience to His major command.

But what does it mean if we refuse to obey the Great Commission? What real life decisions have we made?

It means that we either do not understand Christ's command or that we do understand and are procrastinating, kidding ourselves, or perhaps just willfully disobeying Him. It means that we are selfish, treasuring our own personal comforts and desires above the clear instructions of Christ. It might mean that affluence has lulled us into obsessive self-seeking. Rather than risk some emotional pains, we are willing to let friends go into eternity lost forever without the Savior. It might mean that we have let the worries of the world, the deceitfulness of riches and the desires for other pleasures effectively choke out the Word of God so that it has become silent in our lives.

On the other hand, we must also face the reality of spiritual warfare. Any child of God who is serious about walking with Christ in obedience to the Great Commission will attract the enemy's attention. We live in a satanically-dominated, hostile world surrounded by spiritually blind people. If we step out and obey the Great Commission, Satan will intensify his attacks. Yet our choice to obey opens opportunities for increased joy in the Christian life, the joy of hard-fought battles well won for Christ and for others.

Perhaps you have never thought of your responsibility in these terms. I would like to help you experience the fulfilling excitement of seeing others come to Him. The Bible presents a loving, satisfying, and purposeful lifestyle that will wisely and gently let others know about Christ. Obedience is positive. It does not mean rudeness or foolishness.

We do not have to conduct ourselves so friends flinch every time we come around. It is not necessary to generate the rejections caused by tactless and poorly thought out witnessing efforts. There are ways to share life with friends so that much of the self-inflicted pain can be avoided. This book is designed to help show you how.

To Join the Seeking Heart

The Lord Jesus Christ left heaven and came to earth seeking us. He went to Calvary's cross and conquered death so we can have life. This is the theme of the New Testament, but this truth is the forest which can't be seen because we often settle for a minute inspection of the leaves!

Christ stated His purpose in easily understandable terms: "For the Son of man has come to seek and to save that which was lost" (Luke 19:10).

The word "seek" here has the unmistakable meaning of an active search. The story of Christ's and Zacchaeus's encounter is reported in Luke 19:1-10. It communicates God's method of letting the world know about His Son.

Zacchaeus was wealthy and unpopular, but his heart was hungry for God. None of the professing religious people in Zacchaeus's world cared enough or knew enough to help him know the Lord.

Christ loved Zacchaeus and went where he was. The people of Zacchaeus's day might have found him acceptable if he had turned from his ways, come to their religious meetings, and begged for acceptance on their terms. When Christ went to Zacchaeus's home, the crowd grumbled that He had gone to be the guest of a sinner (v. 7). Christ's action warmly demonstrates His seeking heart. The application is obvious. How many are content to let the Christian life consist of no more than attendance at meetings and devotional exercises? The all-too-average Christian life ends right there. Many fail to encompass others.

Unfortunately, we Christians are clannish. The clique is often our lifestyle. In the name of separation and/or sanctification we have insulated ourselves from those without Jesus Christ. We have created a cloistered group of institutionally domesticated, inward-looking holy huddlers. In our excessive introspection we have become insensitive to those for whom Christ died, as they perish around us.

I am greatly in favor of in-depth Bible study, discipleship, growing in the body, and caring for each other. Any of these good practices, however, can also become an excuse for avoiding the hard work of cultivating a lifestyle which recognizes the major thrust of Christ's message.

There are reasons why this happens. First, spiritual warfare is vicious. The enemy is hard at work to defeat every Christian by implanting certain false notions and priorities. Second, our hearts are deceitful and desperately wicked. We are selfish, as every honest Christian knows. The seeking heart is the healthy, happy, and balanced heart. It produces a successful Christian life. Wherever Christian hearts are seeking, excitement reigns.

But the false visions persist. Christians frequently conjure up all manner of negative images when the Great Commission is mentioned. We see ourselves becoming poverty-stricken. Or we see ourselves turning into miserable people. We think that obeying Christ's commission will result in loss and misery. But Christ promised the opposite. Obeying His command means joy, a great sense of well-being, inner peace, purpose, fulfillment, and abundant life. False visions must not keep us from carrying out our orders.

To Show Others His Love

Christ's Great Commission commands total surrender to His love. "For the love of Christ controls us, having concluded this, that one died for all, therefore all died" (II Cor. 5:14).

All that Christ did, from incarnation to death to resurrection to present intercession, was and is done because He loves us. Christ loves us and asks that we respond in kind. It is not an unreasonable request.

After his denial of Christ, Peter returned to fishing. Christ met him by the shore to restore fellowship. The Lord had only one question, "Simon, son of John, do you love me more than these?" (John 21:15). This is Christ's question to us.

Unless we begin with love for Christ, our activity could be just another exercise in religious duty, or perhaps another conformity to the clique. If, on the other hand, we do His will out of personal devotion to Him, we will be fulfilled now.

Those who are in constant touch with friends who don't yet know Christ live in a world of continuing spiritual challenge. Letting Christ's love flow through us to others for whom He died is the way to a well-rounded, successful Christian life.

To Avoid False Alternatives

Don't get friendship evangelism confused with a frantic, shallow, insensitive, activism. Shallow activism is held up as a model of what a Christian does not want to become, and is used, therefore, as an argument for ignoring those who do not know Christ. The true alternative is winning and discipling people.

Another false choice is full-time ministry or nothing. Some people believe that to become involved with Christ means being a full-time evangelist. But Christ said that all of us are to be witnesses for Him. All of us are witnesses. Some are good, some are bad, some are improving, some, unfortunately, are deteriorating. *Every* believer should make Christ the Lord of his or her life, get to know Him better, diligently study the Bible, develop a prayer life, be Spirit-filled and learn all he or she can about working with, growing with, and helping others in the body of Christ. At the same time, we should be letting Christ's love flow through us to those who do not know Him.

Do not buy the false notion that you must be either a shallow, hyperactive witness or no witness at all while living within the nucleus of the holy huddle. If you live Christ's way, and develop a seeking, caring heart, then you will effectively reach others for Him.

May I Help?

You may genuinely want to reach friends for Christ but do not know how. Or perhaps you have tried but have been discouraged by initial defeat. The emotional pain resulting from rejection cuts deeply. Or perhaps you have given up because of those discouraging false options. The enemy may have you believing there are only two courses: to be rude, aggressively invading the lives of others, or to remain silent. These are not the choices.

You can learn how to be wise, gentle, and effective in speaking to others about Christ. You can learn how to speak with gracious words, seasoned with salt, tailored to fit each person. You can learn to respond to people, not just to their words. You can avoid the pitfall of being quarrelsome and learn to be patient, able to teach, gently correcting those who are in opposition.

If you enter into a pressure-free, loving, seeking lifestyle, the satisfaction is everlasting. Christ will be honored. Fears and obsessive needs for cliques will disappear. Spiritual health and success are the norm for this adventuresome life. Others who might never have known the Savior will be with Him and you forever because you have cared.

2

Yes, You Can

A professional golfer was impressed with the coordination and strength of his friend, a weightlifter who was six feet, six inches tall and weighed 265 pounds. He invited the weightlifter to learn golf. When they played together, the golfer explained how to tee up and drive a ball. On his first attempt, the weightlifter drove the ball well over four hundred yards onto the green. The ball stopped about eighteen inches short of the cup.

They walked to the ball and the weightlifter asked what he should do next.

The golfer replied, "Now you're supposed to putt the ball into that hole."

With a straight face his friend asked, "Why didn't you tell me that back there?"

That kind of self-confidence is admirable. The stronger athlete had good reason for his optimism. His self-evident physical attributes had been proven over and over. In the same way, a Christian can approach life with great self-assurance.

As briefly mentioned in Chapter 1, every child of God is called to confidence. One of the solid reasons for this is our birth to power. Once an individual trusts Christ, the Lord goes to work in his or her life with the great resurrection power that brought Christ from the grave (Eph. 1:18-20). We obviously are not yet in resurrected form. However, one of the major truths of successful Christian living is that while we are still in this frail body the resurrection power of Christ provides the dynamic for us to walk in newness of life (Rom. 6:4). The new birth ushers us into a whole new spectrum of life, balanced with gentleness, power, and love. We have been delivered from the vicious domain of darkness to the kingdom of the Son of God. Our spirit is not one of cringing cowardess, but of power, love, and discipline (II Tim. 1:7).

The sovereign almighty God of the universe loves us dearly. It is inconceivable that He would do anything but good for His children. We may have every confidence that the Lord who gave us His Great Commission has given each of us precisely the gift we need and the power to exercise that gift successfully. These are His promises.

After eighty years of battle and victory, Joshua made one of the most profound observations in Scripture about God's faithfulness: "You know in all your hearts and in all your souls, that not one word of all the good words which the Lord your God spoke concerning you has failed: All have been fulfilled for you, not one of them has failed" (Josh. 23:14).

God will keep His promises to you. Your life can become God's mighty channel for bringing others to the Savior. He will guide you and give you everything you need to overcome your fears.

Understand the Power of Love

Once the power of love is understood and applied, miracles will begin to happen. Unfortunately, we may find ourselves frozen into certain patterns which assure defeat before we start. But once the positive forces of love are put into operation and the negative elements which legalism has injected are deleted, the way can be paved to some fulfilling experiences. I prefer to stress the positive, but in this case must focus on some negatives which are killing Christians' joy.

In some circles Christians are regimented into assorted holy huddles which exclude unbelievers. Certain standards of conduct are the identifying characteristics of good clansmen. If one is to be accepted, there are certain "must-not-do" rules he must follow. Judgmental attitudes begin to grow. These are transmitted to the unbeliever as rejection.

A predictable phenomenon follows. A Christian, exposed to the Bible and good Bible teachers, will become concerned for the unbeliever. Operating under an intense sense of duty, he or she nervously begins an unrealistic approach to the outsider. Defeat is inevitable.

To begin with, the unbeliever senses the harsh judgmental rejection from regimented religious people. The Christian, under the stress of an awkward outreach effort, is operating with detectable apprehension. The relationship already is touchy. The slightest irritant sends it into hopeless argument. No one wins.

The scene changes completely when the atmosphere is saturated with love. The person without Christ senses that the believer is genuinely concerned for his well-being. All the attitudes, conversations, and nonverbal communications indicate a warm desire for friendship. Sensing that he now has a willing listener, the one for whom Christ died will begin to open up.

This loving approach and the predictable reception characterized Paul's life. It was a major reason for his success. During the course of telling the Thessalonians how he came to them (I Thess. 1-2), Paul confirms the power of love. He states his affection for them which made him desire to share not just the gospel but his own life (I Thess. 2:8). As a result, the Thessalonians became imitators of Paul (I Thess. 1:6). This is what every Christian would like to see happen, but it does not happen enough. More people will be receptive to us when they sense that we care.

Years ago the Lord began to teach me some of the truths about friendship evangelism through some pioneers in the field. It was thirty-two years before this writing that I first heard the now familiar concept described as "the bridge of friendship." Once that bridge is built, much can be transported over it. It does not make much difference how many obstacles the unbeliever has or what they are. Friendship's bridge can span most roadblocks to faith. This truth was powerfully demonstrated in the life of a fine Christian woman I know. She earnestly devoted herself to spiritual activities for many years. She was an accomplished Bible teacher and counselor. She consistently served God. In all of her years spent walking with Him, however, she had never introduced anyone to the Savior.

God in His loving grace arranged for our paths to cross. Within a few months she became enthusiastic over the ministry of friendship evangelism. The reason later came out. By learning some basic biblical truths and applying them with love and warm concern for a nonbelieving friend, with whom she had daily contact, she led a young woman to the Savior. A pattern of New Testament friendship evangelism was begun in her life. It soon spread to other lives. Her excitement continues to grow.

Great harvests are reaped when love is sown. Begin planting that crop. Then stand back and watch the miracles begin to happen. You will be living in a new world of productive relationships with unbelieving friends.

Learn Some Answers

> And the Lord's bond-servant must not be quarrelsome, but be kind to all, able to teach, patient when wronged, with gentleness correcting those who are in opposition, if perhaps God may grant them repentance leading to the knowledge of the truth, and they may come to their senses and escape from the snare of the devil, having been held captive by him to do his will (II Tim. 2:24-26).

This is one of the key passages about communicating with those who do not have Christ. This passage underscores the truth that we are commanded to learn answers to the questions non-Christians ask. We must be able to teach and gently correct those who are in opposition. This requires information.

Peter adds that we always should be ready to have an answer for anyone who asks us to give an account for the hope that is in us. We must respond with gentleness and reverence (I Peter 3:15).

Most Christians can learn, within a relatively short period of time, to answer over 90 percent of the questions any unbeliever will ask. A number of excellent works on the subject are available. I suggest Paul Little's *How to Give Away Your Faith*, Chapter 5, and his book, *Know Why You Believe*.

In my many years of friendship evangelism, I have found witnessing tactics that have proven effective. I hope they encourage you. Please seriously consider them for your personal use. Other believers who are neither gifted evangelists nor formally trained in the Bible have also found success with them.

One of the major questions raised by those without Christ concerns the reliability of the Bible. Closely related is the issue of Christ's being the only way to God. Both rest on the credentials of Christ and the Bible.

Review the Evidence

The ultimate question is whether Jesus Christ is the true Son of God. To determine if He is true, we need to look at His credentials in comparison with the credentials of all others, including ourselves. This is the beginning point. We will have made a major contribution to an individual's life if we can help him or her think in terms of the reliability of Christ's teachings. Here is some of the evidence for Christ.

Fulfilled Prophecy

Fulfilled prophecy constitutes one of the major and more dramatic evidences for Christ and the Bible. Statistics vary, but there are about three hundred prophecies about Christ. Over fifty of these are major prophecies. You can find lists of them in good Bible handbooks and in other sources such as Josh McDowell's *Evidence that Demands a Verdict*.

The following prophecies have to do with things which could not have been arranged by Christ Himself. Here are some of the major fulfilled prophecies about Christ.

- Jesus would be born at Bethlehem (Mic. 5:2; Matt. 2:1, 6; Luke 2:1-10).
- Jesus' family would travel to Egypt (Hos. 11:1; Matt. 2:15).
- Herod would kill young children (Jer. 31:15; Matt 2:16-18).
- Jesus would enter Jerusalem on a donkey (Zech. 9:9; Luke 19:35-37).
- Jesus would be betrayed by a friend (Ps. 41:9; 55:12-14; Matt. 10:4).
- Jesus would be betrayed for thirty pieces of silver (Zech. 11:12-13; Matt. 26:15; 27:9-10).
- The betrayal money would be thrown in God's house (Zech. 11:13b; Matt. 27:5a).
- The betrayal money would be given for a potter's field (Zech. 11:13b; Matt. 27:7).
- Jesus would be forsaken by His disciples (Zech. 13:7; Mark 14:50).
- Jesus would be wounded and bruised (Isa. 53:5; Matt. 27:26).
- Jesus would be beaten and spit upon (Isa. 50:6; Matt. 26:67).
- Jesus would be mocked (Ps. 22:7-8; Matt. 27:31).
- Jesus' hands and feet would be pierced (Ps. 22:16; Luke 23:33; 24:39).

- Jesus would die with malefactors (Isa. 53:9, 12; Matt. 27:38).
- Jesus' clothing would be divided and lots cast for it (Ps. 22:18; John 19:23-24).
- Jesus would suffer thirst (Ps. 22:15; John 19:28).
- Gall and vinegar would be offered to Jesus (Ps. 69:21; Matt. 27:34).
- Jesus' dying words were foretold (Ps. 22:1; 31:5; Matt. 27:46; Mark 15:34; Luke 23:46).
- Not a bone of Jesus' body would be broken (Ps. 34:20; John 19:33).
- Jesus' side would be pierced (Zech. 12:10; John 19:34, 37).
- A rich man would bury Jesus (Isa. 53:9; Matt. 27:57-60).

Often unbelievers argue that the timing and place of Christ's birth allowed Him the opportunity to make the most of the prevailing Jewish messianic expectations. As a single argument this is remotely feasible. However, it would be most difficult for Christ while hanging on the cross to have arranged fulfillment for other prophecies such as the gambling for His clothing. Moreover, modern scholarship and archaeology consistently reaffirm the existence of the prophecies before Christ was born. It is logically unrealistic to consider that the prophecies were fulfilled by coincidence.

The odds that only eight of those major prophecies could be fulfilled by coincidence are given by McDowell in his *Evidence that Demands a Verdict*.[1] Imagine that the entire state of Texas is covered with silver dollars two feet thick.

1. McDowell, Josh, *Evidence that Demands a Verdict*, (San Bernardino, CA: Campus Crusade for Christ, Inc.), 1972, p. 175.

One of these billions of silver dollars is marked, and someone is blindfolded and given one chance to go into Texas and pick up the marked coin at random. His chances of picking up the marked coin have the same odds that McDowell attributes to eight of these prophecies being fulfilled by chance! Any honest reflection on fulfilled prophecies should be open to the most logical conclusion: they were inspired by God.

Archaeological Confirmation

Archaeology is another major source of evidence which continues to verify the accuracy of Scripture. Archaeological evidence abounds. In days gone by, critics alleged that Moses could not have written the Ten Commandments and other items of law given by God because his contemporary culture was not advanced enough. Then discoveries such as King Tutankhamen's tomb were made. Artifacts from King Tutankhamen's tomb obviously reflect a highly articulate, sophisticated culture. King Tutankhamen came within a century of Moses, from the same household.

Daniel 5:29 reports Belshazzar's vesting Daniel with authority as third ruler in the kingdom. This provided a field day for the critics for many years. Belshazzar was unknown to them. Their position was that any knowledgeable person should recognize that Nabonidus was the last king of Babylon. Then archaeologists dug up inscriptions by Nabonidus that refer to his son, Belshazzar. Daniel 5:29, therefore, is impeccably accurate in referring to Daniel not as second but as third ruler in the kingdom.

As the modern science and art of archaeology has developed, that which objectively substantiates the Bible has increased. W. F. Albright of Johns Hopkins University is a well-known name in the field of Palestinian archaeology. In discussing the contents of the Pentateuch he says, "New discoveries continue to confirm the historical accuracy or the literary antiquity of detail after detail in it."[2]

In a later review of archaeological confirmation of biblical history Albright says, "In the foregoing chapters we have had occasion to mention many examples where the facts brought to light by Palestinian archaeology agree with specific points in Biblical history."[3]

It is of more than passing interest that a scholar of Albright's magnitude would refer to "many examples," wherein Palestinian archaeology has reinforced the credibility of biblical history. Albright's many examples can be read with great delight for they serve to strengthen personal faith.

Albright makes an additional assertion which gives special impact to the major problem of skepticism. For some unusual reasons (which the Bible explains) it seems highly desirable in certain circles to reject the Bible. This is done in spite of massive objective, logical, intelligent evidence to the contrary. Albright's comment is interesting: "Biblical historical data are accurate to an extent far surpassing the ideas of any modern critical students, who have consistently tended to err on the side of hypercriticism."[4]

This particular Albright work has been used as a specific illustration of the basic truth that archaeology, which gives evidence we can see, touch, and photograph, confirms the accuracy of the Bible in many details.

Considerable literature describes additional massive archaeological verification of Scripture. For more detailed

2. Albright, W. F., *The Archaeology of Palestine*, (Magnolia, MA: Peter Smith Publishing, Inc.), 1971, p. 225.

3. *Ibid.*, p. 227.

4. *Ibid.*, p. 229.

discussions see Yamauchi's *The Stones and the Scriptures*, Barton's *Archaeology and the Bible*, works by Unger, Kenyon, Thompson, Free, Vos, and the archaeology sections in Bible dictionaries (*Zondervan's Pictorial*, *Unger's*, *The New Bible Dictionary*) and handbooks (Unger's, Halley's, and Eerdmans') and in some study Bibles such as the *Open Bible*. A helpful new family of literature has appeared since the discovery of the Dead Sea Scrolls, such as Menahem Mansoor's textbook, *The Dead Sea Scrolls*.

These books will give you ample credible evidence with which to deal with those who dismiss the Bible as being full of "myth and superstition." Time and time again, archaeological discoveries have substantiated the Bible's historical accuracy. This, of course, does not ultimately determine its uniquely divine origin. It does, however, add to the mountain of evidence that the Bible is more than just another book.

Christ's Universal Appeal

A third area of evidence is the most overwhelming to me as a trial lawyer. That is Christ's universal appeal. Whether it be the Borneo headhunter, the American businessman, the Amazonian Aborigine, the European sophisticate, the African nationalist, or the awakened Oriental, Christ has met their deepest needs. He can satisfy the need of any heart at any level of any culture that comes to Him on His terms. He is unique in all of human history.

Your friend might remonstrate, thinking of those who have been disappointed in their religious experience. Try to discover the reason for the disappointment. Please notice the qualifying condition: all must come to Christ on *His terms*. Almost everyone has been disappointed at one time or another in religious institutions (and in all institutions for that matter). We have been disappointed in other human beings and in associations of human beings. Many have been disappointed in some false god in which they believed. But Christ satisfies the individual who comes to Him as the incarnate, crucified, resurrected Son of God who lives to make intercession for His own. Anyone who has come, acknowledging that all have sinned, that no one can be saved by good works, that Christ alone has made the payment satisfactory to take away our sins, and thus has believed and received Christ as Savior, has found that Jesus Christ has forgiven sins and gives life everlasting. He also finds that Christ makes life in all of its fullness available to each of His own now. Life is enjoyed here and now to the degree the individual child of God decides to walk in fellowship with Him.

100 Percent Success

Closely allied to Christ's universal appeal is His 100 percent track record. Christ has done everything He promised to do for everyone who trusted Him on His terms. Not only has His appeal been universal, it has been successful every time any person has received Him. Obviously, no mere human being can claim 100 percent success. We all fail on occasion, even at that which we do best.

Changed Lives

Christ changes all kinds of lives for the better when people trust Him. People trapped in the humdrum of life find meaning in Christ. Those swept along in the rat race learn what true inner repose is. Shattered homes are mended. Excitement replaces boredom. In more dramatic instances, the alcoholic is made whole and the former prostitute radiates the holy love of Christ.

A compelling evidence for Christ's life-changing power is the accumulated weight of well-being reflected in so many "average" lives. Christ gives people answers where before there were only questions. He gives light where there was darkness, fullness for emptiness, and purpose instead of mere survival. He works where we live, in the increasingly difficult stress of everyday life.

We are being made aware of the dramatic changes Christ has brought about in famous political personalities. And former mobsters, alcoholics, and drug addicts have become shining witnesses for Him. They give Christ all the glory.

To any logical, honest, objective, intelligent mind, the evidence for Christ is imposing enough to be worthy of consideration. To the mind open to faith, the evidence is compelling. Christ is God.

The Resurrection of Christ

Christ's resurrection is the ultimate determinative issue. There are only two options. Christ either did or did not rise from the grave. The evidence that He did is overwhelming.

In addition to the contemporary evidence for Christ, history offers substantiating proof. It cannot be repeated for laboratory observation, but does give compelling corroboration. For example, I cannot prove to you that I went to work last Friday. That is history and has been accomplished. But I offer historical evidence. There are witnesses who can tell you where I was. In addition to witnesses there are other objective facts which would indicate that I was at work, such as dated letters. The fact that something happened in history and cannot be repeated for observation does not invalidate its truth.

History's best evidence speaks convincingly for the resurrection. Christ's tomb was empty. It was in the area controlled by the hostile opposition and was guarded by men under penalty of death if the body was removed. The early church almost completely disregarded the empty tomb, behavior that would be directly in contrast to normal reverence for the resting place of a dead leader. Since Christ rose from the dead, however, it was not the tomb but the living Lord with whom they were preoccupied.

The New Testament is a minutely accurate historical record. The biographers of Christ record the whole truth, even elements unfavorable to themselves. Nothing else in their writings or lives indicates that they were frauds. Why then would they lie about the most important single event, the resurrection?

The apostles were a miserable discouraged group of unlikely religious leaders after the death of Christ. They had experienced what seemed to be three and one-half years of failure. Within a very few days they completely changed, becoming firebrands who changed the course of history. Why? Sufficient time had not passed for either an adequate fraud or legend. The most logical explanation is the resurrection of Christ.

These apostles also gave their lives for the faith. All were killed for their faith except John who was exiled. Intelligent men do not die for a fraud. Some people admittedly will die for a cause even though it is false. Human nature can be motivated to reach such extremities. However, these men lived the way they did because of personal observation and contact with the resurrected Christ. They experienced immediate success which has continued to this day. The resurrected Christ is the only logical explanation.

Concentrate on Offering Loving Help, Not on Winning Arguments

Once you have intelligent answers to the unbeliever's questions, you can accomplish your goals. But it is not a question of winning arguments. What really takes place has far more meaning in human relationships. First, your entire demeanor will indicate that you genuinely care. You are making an effort to do something in love.

Next, the unbeliever will see that there are logical, objective, honest, and intelligent reasons for the Christian faith. We know that Christ is the only way. No one else has conquered the grave. Thus, we have a Savior who is entirely different from every other religious leader who ever lived. He has answers, not just opinions. He has conquered the ultimate enemy, death. The evidence is overwhelming that Christ is true. Therefore, the believer is operating on solid ground.

Finally, your self-confidence will become contagious. You have a worthy object of faith and you know why you believe in Christ. The unbeliever can only come to a conclusion that without Christ, he simply cannot know. So you can communicate a confidence which a person without Christ can never know. But be careful: arrogance and self-righteousness are not attractive.

In some cases, at this point, the subjective smoke screens will be blown away. The emotional and intellectual defense mechanisms will have been removed. The unbeliever will be open to listen to the message of Christ. Now you can become the beautiful feet that carry the Good News.

3

The Beautiful Feet

Three people were seated at a restaurant table. Two were very slim. One was not so slim. The slim ones drank unsweetened tea. In front of the not-so-slim one was a seven-dip, hot fudge, marshmallow, whipped cream, nuts, and cherry covered calorie monster. Just before digging in, the not-so-slim one said, "I have tried calorie counting and I have tried crash diets; I have tried jogging and I have tried isometrics. Now I am trying for the heavyweight championship of the world."

Unfortunately, some who know Christ have given up without ever trying to be the beautiful feet who bring the Good News to others. Do not give up. You can learn to do it well.

Before attempting to lead anyone to Christ, you should know how you are going to do it. I am convinced that many more Christians would lead friends to Christ if they knew how to "close the deal." Technically, this chapter might belong to Part Two since it deals with the most vital part of what we will do on the outside. However, you must be internally prepared by knowing how to lead someone to Christ before that important transaction can take place. It is also included here to help build self-confidence. Lack of understanding in this area is another sad cause of defeat for many Christians before they get started. Hopefully then, learning how to lead another to Christ will begin with a constructive change in you.

Begin the Beautiful Quest

"How beautiful are the feet of those who bring glad tidings of good things!" (Rom. 10:15b).

Romans 10:13-15 presents the Great Commission imperative in a searching way. It should touch the heart of any sensitive child of God.

Verse 13 contains the eternal promise of salvation to all who call upon the Lord. Then in four rhetorical questions, Paul gives the challenge: "How then shall they call upon Him in whom they have not believed? And how shall they believe in Him whom they have not heard? And how shall they hear without a preacher? And how shall they preach, unless they are sent?" (Rom. 10:14-15a).

Then follows the eternal statement concerning the beautiful feet. The Greek word *beautiful* means that which is seasonable, produced at the right time. It is used to speak of the exquisite beauty of ripe fruits.

People all around us are looking for meaning. The world is full of shattered dreams, wounded hearts, broken lives, and wasted talents. Hearts are struggling in darkness for fulfillment. People without Christ grow old, decay, and die without God, without hope, and without meaning. We hold the key to fulfillment now and to paradise forever. We have the Good News. We can introduce people to the One who is the Light of the world. He can bring fulfillment to each one.

The apple tree has no ultimate meaning until it brings forth the apple. Human lives will never bring forth what was intended until they know Jesus Christ. They will never know Him without us.

We must follow biblical principles. If we are controlled by love (II Cor. 5:14), if we use wisdom in relating to those who are without Christ (Col. 4:5), if we tailor our speech to the individual with whom we are relating (see Chapter 8), and if we lovingly extend the invitation (see Chapter 10), then we can anticipate God's working in power through our lives.

In the following pages you will find some scriptural steps for leading people to Christ. These steps work for most believers; they do not depend on individual gifts or style. They are designed to help as you rub shoulders with friends during everyday life. Other good methods are available, and you may also want to try them. Which method you use is not important. It is vital that you have a way to lead someone to Christ and that you know how to use it.

Build a Friendship

It may take five minutes, five days, five months, or five years, but a bridge of friendship can be built in most cases. Not everyone with whom you cultivate a friendship will trust Christ for salvation, but more will listen to you than to a stranger. You must take some initiative. Choose the people you have the best opportunities to be a witness to and begin praying for each individual. Then spend time with them. Have lunch together or go out for coffee.

Be a good listener. Do not worry about bringing up the subject. (More details about how to do this are dealt with in the suggested experiment at the end of Chapter 9.) Because you genuinely care, the power of love will have its warming influence in the lives you will be touching. People respond to that kind of outreach.

Do not overlook the necessity of this continuing personal contact. It is vital. All the rest is mere gimmickry without it. Share your life because you want to, and your friends will feel your genuine concern without a word being spoken. Christ spent a lot of time doing this (John 14:9; 15:15) as did Paul.

Step Through the Open Door

Strategic guiding principles are found in Colossians 4:2-6. One is praying for the open door. As you do that, take an active part in wisely providing for the opportunity. It is biblical to use wisdom and sound judgment (Col. 4:5; Rom. 12:3). Make an effort to get alone with the one in whom you are interested. Generally, individuals will speak more freely about important personal matters in a one-on-one situation.

Let the other person initiate the general subject of Christianity if at all possible. At this point you will be faced with one of the two most difficult obstacles to overcome in leading a person to Christ. Unfortunately, most believers are defeated at one or both of these points. The first is bringing up the subject, and the second is consummating the transaction when the individual actually receives Christ. The spiritual warfare is ever present, but by the grace of God, you can succeed. Eventually this will become enjoyable.

Pay a Genuine Compliment

During your time together, spiritual matters will have been discussed between you and your friend. It should be possible for you to honestly pay a compliment. It might be simply to recognize his or her genuine interest in God.

The point, of course, is to serve the individual in any way possible so he or she can have the opportunity to receive Christ as his or her own. Christ taught that if the Holy Spirit is convicting people concerning sin, then they will be aware of sin because they have not believed in Him (John 16:9). Therefore, if we focus on personal belief in Christ, we are in harmony with the convicting ministry of the Spirit in the heart of the one to whom we are bringing the Good News. In view of this truth, I try to structure my compliment, if it can be done genuinely (and please note the stress on genuineness), around appropriation of Christ.

We must be careful never to mislead anyone or to put words in a person's mouth. I compliment a person on an interest in the Lord when it can be honestly done. If possible, I go further and say something like this: "It is not right to put words in your mouth, and I don't want to do that, but may I give you my impression of where you are? May I let you know how you are coming across to me? As far as I can tell, I believe you want to be sure Christ is yours. Do you?"

If the answer is "yes," then an effort can be made to lead the person to Christ. If the answer is "no" or "I do not know," then it is possible to ask why and answer some more questions, helping him move a step or two closer to the Savior.

Do not put yourself under a lot of pressure. Without necessarily trying to lead someone to Christ, deal only with this first serious obstacle, bringing up the subject. Once you have spent a few hours with a person, gotten alone with him and responded to his initiative, you may be amazed at what a sincere compliment can do.

Give an Understanding of the Gospel

In Colossians 4:4 Paul asked his fellow believers to pray that he would make the gospel clear. It is a mistake to assume that anyone understands the gospel. Most people do not. The natural man cannot receive the things of God unless the Spirit reveals them to Him (I Cor. 2:14). Go through it one point at a time to be sure it is understood. I suggest using the most familiar verse in the Bible, John 3:16, as your guide.

Reaffirm that the individual has told you that he wants to be sure Christ is his Savior. Then let him tell you what he believes by answering a few questions. If he believes these basics, then he can be sure that he has eternal life upon reception of Christ. Ask questions about John 3:16. You can follow this order:[1]

> *"For God so loved the world . . ."*
> Do you believe that everything Jesus did in leaving heaven, dying on the cross, and conquering death was accomplished because He loves you personally?

Wait for a verbal answer. If the response to this or any of the following questions is "no" or "I'm not sure," then you can ask why and continue the conversation. If the in-

1. The following material is taken from "The Gift," (Knoxville, TN, New Life, Inc.), 1980, and is used by permission.

dividual is reluctant, do not force the issue. However, remember that intense spiritual warfare begins in almost every case when someone gets serious about trusting Christ. You will need to help the person proceed.

You can use these substantiating truths. Tell the person that because of His love, God wants him to experience total fulfillment. "I came that they might have life, and might have it abundantly" (John 10:10b). Let the person know that God wants him to be saturated with a great sense of well-being. "These things I have spoken to you, that My joy may be in you, and that your joy may be made full" (John 15:11). Remind your friend that God wants him to have everlasting life. "For God so loved the world, that He gave His only begotten Son, that whoever believes in Him should not perish, but have eternal life" (John 3:16).

". . . that He gave His only begotten Son . . ."
Do you believe that Jesus Christ was God's Son, and that when He died on the cross He paid the debt for all of our sins?

God says that our sins have separated us from Him and that no one is good enough by his own effort and in his own merit to please God. Only Christ's death on the cross paid the debt for all our sins and guarantees acceptance with God. ". . . and He Himself bore our sins in His body on the cross, that we might die to sin and live to righteousness; for by His wounds you were healed" (I Peter 2:24). "In Him we have redemption through His blood, the forgiveness of our trespasses, according to the riches of His grace" (Eph. 1:7).

". . . that whoever believes in Him should not perish . . ."
Do you believe that you have sinned against God and will perish if you do not receive Christ as your Savior?

Every human being has sinned and falls short of the standard God requires. "For all have sinned, and fall short of the glory of God" (Rom. 3:23).

God is love, but God also is holy and must punish evil. All rebellion to Him is destructive and requires judgment. "For the wages of sin is death; but the free gift of God is eternal life in Christ Jesus our Lord" (Rom. 6:23).

". . . but have eternal life."
Do you believe that Christ keeps His promises and will give you eternal life if you receive Him as your Savior?

Eternal life is a gift of God to be received by personally believing in Jesus Christ. "But as many as received Him, to them He gave the right to become children of God, even to those who believe in His name" (John 1:12).

Christ conquered death in His resurrection. This demonstrated His power and ability as the Son of God to guarantee eternal life to all who receive Him. "That Christ died for our sins according to the Scriptures, and that He was buried, and that He was raised on the third day according to the Scriptures" (I Cor. 15:3b-4).

Give an Invitation

If your friend has said yes to all the previous questions, then he believes everything he needs in order to become God's child. He can have eternal life by receiving Jesus Christ. Say to him, "You are invited to receive Christ now. Will you?"

Lead in a Prayer of Acceptance

Assure your friend that God is listening and wants to make him His child. Remind your friend that when he talks to the Lord, he must be sure to receive Jesus Christ as Lord and Savior. God will keep His promise and give him eternal life. Have him pray with his own words or with this prayer:

Thank you, Lord Jesus, for loving me, for dying for all my sins, and for conquering death. Confessing that I have sinned and deserve only judgment without you, I now receive you as my Savior and Lord. Thank you for forgiving all my sins and for giving me life everlasting.

In most cases this is the most difficult part of leading one to Christ. Offer to pray first, encouraging your friend to pray out loud after you. Emphasize that he must receive Christ. Doubts sometimes grow out of a vague prayer. The person later remembers that he desired some sort of commitment, but is not sure of what happened. Stress that whatever else he tells the Lord, he should clearly say that he is receiving Christ. If he does not know what to pray but sincerely means what is written in the above prayer, then God knows his heart and surely will receive him if he simply reads the prayer to the Lord.

After praying together, immediately give help with assurance. Ask your friend what would happen if he or she died that day. If Christ keeps His promises, then we can be sure that we will be with Him forever. We do not have to hope so or depend on any subsequent event to make us His child. Give your friend this information.

Give Assurance

Remind the new believer that since He has received Christ, God has kept His promise and has made him His child. Your friend presently possesses eternal life. Let him know that his assurance of eternal life depends on the promise of God, not on feelings. "These things I have written to you who believe in the name of the Son of God, in order that you may know that you have eternal life" (I John 5:13). Feelings can be deceitful, and human experience varies with circumstances. Doubts may come. Remember that God's faithfulness never changes, and He will never reject anyone who comes to Him through Christ. ". . . the one who comes to Me I will certainly not cast out" (John 6:37b).

Christ promises that having received Him your friend is now His child and will never come into judgment. "Truly, truly, I say to you, he who hears My word, and believes Him who sent Me, has eternal life, and does not come into judgment, but has passed out of death into life" (John 5:24).

Stress the Importance of Growth.

It is important that each new believer recognizes Christ as Lord and grows in his or her new spiritual life. ". . . but grow in the grace and knowledge of our Lord and Savior Jesus Christ" (II Peter 3:18a).

Encourage the new child of God to cultivate a personal fellowship with Christ and to learn to love Him. This is done through a proper attitude of yieldedness to Christ, Bible reading, prayer, and fellowship with other Christians. He should become active in a Christ-honoring church.

The Lord instructed us to make disciples, not converts. Conversion is not the end; it is the beginning. The individual needs to become a child who delights Father, enjoys life in all of its fullness, and who can learn to share the faith with others.

4

You Should Know
Where I'm Coming From

My father was one of the finest practical psychologists I have ever known, although he was a professional educator. He taught me the importance of positive attitudes.

Once when he was principal of a large high school in Jacksonville, Florida, one of the students went on the warpath. He was a large young man nicknamed Moose. Moose had dropped out of school that day and was lashing out at those around him. He came to the high school to attack my father.

My father walked out onto one of the porches behind the school, and Moose was standing there crouched like an animal ready to spring, shifting his weight from foot to foot. My father immediately assumed an attitude of compassion and concern for Moose's well-being. He said, "Moose, I know they are after you, and they're headed this way. I believe if you will go that way (pointing), you'll be able to get away from them."

Moose blinked his eyes, not understanding. For what seemed like an eternity he was undecided. Father repeated his advice. Moose jumped the porch railing and ran in the suggested direction.

What if my father had met Moose with hostility? The results would have been disastrous. Attitude made the difference.

This episode illustrates one of the basic differences between success and failure in the Christian witness. Attitudes determine our relationships with the Lord, with each other, and with unbelievers, and they also determine what we do in all of those relationships.

Forming Our Own Attitudes

Mental health disciplines are turning more and more to the truth that we are in control of our wills. For too long we have passed the buck to heredity and environment. Intellect, emotions, and will all have a role in the way we form attitudes. Some people are smarter than others, but each normal person has the ability to receive and evaluate information.

We are, however, primarily emotional beings. Much of what we are emotionally and mentally has grown out of our relationships with others, especially those of childhood. Many times we are victims of emotions but need not be. By exercising proper responsibility we can avoid being enslaved by negative emotions.

The will is in our control. Every mentally competent person regularly exercises the will. What clothes will we wear? What food will we eat? What recreation will we choose? We make countless decisions as part of the daily living process.

No one needs to be rendered spiritually unfruitful because of negative emotions. The will can be controlled by godly exercise. Proper attitudes can result in proper decisions, which, in turn, produce a loving, receptive atmosphere. These attitudes greatly affect how others respond to us.

What is our attitude toward Christ's Great Commission? We can obey or disobey, and stagnation in the holy huddle's embrace is disobedience. "If you love Me, you will keep My commandments" (John 14:15). "And by this we know that we have come to know Him, if we keep His commandments" (I John 2:3). We talk a lot about our Lord and Savior and our attitudes toward Him. If we genuinely love Christ, then we will keep His commandments. He commands us to believe, to take the Good News to others, and to love each other as He loved us.

The satanic philosophy which originated sin was self-will. Christ redeemed the world when He came and said, "Not my will, but thine be done." Rebellion against God is the very heart of sin. Satan's philosophy has saturated the world. The worst attitude a Christian can have (disobedience to God) is perfectly acceptable in this evil system. We constantly must guard our hearts to be sure we are following Christ's attitude and not the enemy's.

Most of us have been hurt emotionally when rejected in efforts to talk with others about the Lord. In the spiritual warfare there is invariably a price to pay for victory. In the middle of the enemy's opposition, however, each child of God can make a decision. We are in control of our wills and can obey God because we love Him. The resulting joy of battles hard-fought and well-won is much more pleasant than the agony of willful cowardice. For those willing to obey, the battle soon becomes a fulfilling adventure.

Our Attitudes Toward the Unbeliever

One without Christ is a victim of the enemy, not the enemy (II Cor. 4:3-4; II Tim. 2:25-26).

The unbeliever must see the love of Christ in us if he or she is to see it anywhere. As mentioned previously, His love should control our lives. "For the love of Christ controls us, having concluded this, that one died for all, therefore all died" (II Cor. 5:14). With our will, we can decide that we will allow Christ to control us. It is often difficult to love others the way we should. The miracle-working power of the indwelling Spirit of God provides all we need for this. One part of the fruit of the Spirit is love (Gal. 5:22-23). If we walk in the Spirit (confessing any known sins), and make Christ Lord of our lives, then His love will begin to flow through us.

Christ came to seek and to save the lost (Luke 19:10). To share Christ's seeking heart is to search for those who are without. Initial motivation, however, can dwindle in the daily routine. A person with a seeking heart will not offensively impress others with his superior spiritual knowledge. What should come through is warm personal concern.

Christians often are insecure in their faith. Sometimes this insecurity is due to lack of information, sometimes to lack of maturity, and sometimes to lack of fellowship with Christ. A child of God may feel threatened by the entrance of an unbeliever into his or her life. We need to get beyond ourselves and to let Christ teach us how to love. We are His gift to those who are without Him. If we go to them controlled by Christ's love, they will sense our genuine concern for their well-being.

Frequently Christians live in a fantasy world. We believe that those without Christ are having a lot of fun, that they are successful in everything they attempt, that they have all of the things in this life that we do not have. We imagine that they enjoy sin. Our enemy is a clever deceiver.

The contrary is true. The one who has Jesus Christ has the answers. We have available to us life in all of its fullness right now. Satisfaction, peace, love, joy, fulfillment, purpose, power, and a place in the family of God are ours as joint heirs with Jesus Christ. We are on our way to heaven. Unbelievers need us. We should not feel threatened by them.

> And calling them to Himself, Jesus said to them, "You know that those who are recognized as rulers of the Gentiles lord it over them; and their great men exercise authority over them. But it is not so among you, but whoever wishes to become great among you shall be your servant; and whoever wishes to be first among you shall be slave of all. For even the Son of Man did not come to be served, but to serve, and to give His life a ransom for many" (Mark 10:42-45).

Far from feeling threatened, we should learn Christ's attitude of willing service. He gave His life as a ransom for many. We in turn are to serve Him, each other, and those who are enslaved by Satan (II Cor. 4:5). For years, institutionalized Christianity in many ways has looked like an enslaving organization. Outsiders view us as wanting to get their money, to confine them with rules of conduct, and to smother the spark of individuality. These are satanic lies. Unfortunately, they find reason for existence in comfortable cliques and religious counterfeits. Thus, it is all the more imperative that we lovingly seek ways to serve those without Christ.

Two individuals might speak identical words. The words can be absolutely true. One will be listened to under any given set of circumstances; the other will be ignored. The difference is the speaker's attitude. If the person without Christ senses a receptive spirit, he will respond. In most cases, it will only be a question of time, and usually not too much time, until Christ is discussed.

Our Sense of Urgency

Luke 15:1-10 tells two of Christ's parables. Both involve losses: one a sheep; one a coin. The shepherd concentrates all of his efforts on finding the one lost sheep. When it is found there is great joy for the shepherd, for his friends, and for the heavenly host.

If we believe in God, we should live with a daily sense of urgency about the condition of those without Christ. If we fail to win them, they will perish in eternal torment without Christ. Unbelievers are all around us, waiting for us to care enough to tell them the Good News.

One day I invited everyone in my Sunday school class who was not sure if he or she was a Christian to talk with me privately. I had once imagined I stood behind the great white throne looking over Christ's shoulder as members of my class appeared before Him to be assigned to hell forever. I couldn't stand the thought and thus aggressively sought to be sure that all had Christ as their Savior. I labored under God's sense of urgency (John 3:36). A fifty-year-old man responded that day and accepted Christ as his Savior. Within a year and a half he was killed in a head-on collision.

By contrast, during that same time period, another friend came to talk about a great gift he felt he had: he could make people feel good. He wanted to know if that was conversion. He even found that he could make women feel good with his lovemaking. I advised him clearly that this was not of God and that it was not a conversion. What he was doing was making some people feel good temporarily. I tried to point out how great it would be for him to receive Christ. If Christ came into his life, He could share Christ with others and could help them have life everlasting, and they would experience Christ's full joy forever. The man refused. For over an hour, I begged him to receive Christ. I even asked if it would make any difference if I got on my knees and begged. He said no, that he did not want Christ as his Savior. Within sixty days he and his wife were involved in a bizarre situation. He was shot through the eye and the heart. Death came instantly.

Scare tactics are not attractive. All I am interested in is truth. Is Scripture true? Is Christ the Son of God? Is any person just one breath from eternity? Must all have Christ or perish? If so, then we should develop a sense of urgency.

A number of years ago, my brother and I were visiting in Ankara, Turkey, on a business trip. During the course of that visit, our host took us to the tomb of Attaturk, the father of modern Turkey. Attaturk had accomplished amazing things. Some of his favorite books were displayed among his mementos. One portion which had been translated into English captured my attention. It went something like this: "History makes no excuse for the man who is unprepared when opportunity presents itself."

People near us are perishing without Christ. We are living in days of unparalleled openness to the message of Jesus Christ. People are receptive. We need to have a sense of urgency about taking the message to them.

Jeremiah vividly lamented the missed day of opportunity. "Harvest is past, summer is ended, and we are not saved" (Jer. 8:20).

Paul knew that today is all we have. Tomorrow may never come. "And working together with Him, we also urge you not to receive the grace of God in vain;—for He says, 'At the acceptable time I listened to you, and on the day of salvation I helped you'; behold, now is 'the acceptable time.' behold, now is 'the day of salvation' " (II Cor. 6:1-2).

The New Testament closes with a message of urgency. The time will come when those who are filthy will still be filthy and those who are righteous will still be righteous (Rev. 22:11). As God finishes His written Word to man, He extends the final urgent invitation to come and take the water of life without cost (Rev. 22:17).

5

I Didn't Notice

How sensitive are we to Christ and to the desperate condition of those without Him? What set of values governs our lives? Do we see the primary issues from God's point of view?

A story from the film-making industry involves a famous producer. He was working on the biggest scene of his most spectacular production, a battle involving one hundred thousand foot soldiers, fifteen thousand cavalry, five thousand camels, and four hundred elephants. In order to assure thorough coverage, cameramen were set up at three strategic locations. Charlie was at the edge of the action on the desert, Sam was well-entrenched in the middle, and Ed was on a cliff.

The producer made certain that everyone was in place and called for action. The infantry battled against each other. The cavalry charged and countercharged. Dust clouds gathered. Camels galloped, and elephants stampeded.

When it was all done, the producer and his associates went to Charlie, asking how filming went from the edge of the battleground. Charlie answered, "What pictures? A half dozen camels got away, knocked me over, and destroyed my equipment. I don't have one foot of film." The producer responded, "That's all right. That's why we have Sam in the middle and Ed on the cliff. We're covered from every angle."

They looked for Sam. Tragedy had struck. Somehow a cavalry charge had come straight into the bunker, destroying it and him. Sam and all of his equipment were trampled into the desert sands.

Confident that his man on the cliff was above any danger, the producer went to the foot of the precipice and called out, "How did it go, Ed?" Ed waved enthusiastically, looked down and said, "Anytime you're ready, I'll roll 'em!"

It seems almost impossible for any Christian to miss the charge of Jesus Christ to the church. We are to go to those without Him. Christ has sent us. We do not have an assortment of commissions; we have only one Great Commission. Are we still waiting for the action when we long since should have been part of it?

Once before speaking at an evangelical seminary, I made an effort to get acquainted with some of the students. During part of this fellowship I wound up taking two of the students out for a cup of coffee. We were discussing faith, our Lord, and what our emphasis should be as bearers of varied gifts working together in the body of Christ.

These young men did not recognize the Great Commission as a priority. I tried to convince them that the whole church of Jesus Christ is responsible to obey His Commission. Everyone is a witness. The New Testament stresses that every gift should be used to obey Christ and, more particularly, to see that His main business is getting done—namely, taking the gospel to every creature in the world. This is the reason Christ died—so that people could be saved.

One of the students had a troubled look on his face. Shrugging his shoulders in apparent confusion, he said that he did not believe everyone should be involved in the Great Commission. He thought that our primary purpose was to "become more Christlike." I agreed with him 100 percent. Then I asked a question which helped him to see a new dimension. Christ said, as recorded in Luke 19:10, that He came to seek and to save the lost. If a child of God is becoming more Christlike, then what kind of a heart will he have? Obviously, a seeking heart—seeking those without the Savior.

I believe with all my heart that our primary obligation is to worship and glorify the Lord. We also are to love one another. However, His great charge to the church still stands as our major responsibility as believers joined together by the Holy Spirit of God. We are to go.

What Is Our Problem?

Our problem is the sinful nature which is a part of every Christian. We must contend with it daily. The human race has been blinded by Satan (II Cor. 4:2-4). A child of God does not lose that sinful nature when he receives Christ. He receives a new nature which is to be cultivated so that it dominates our lives. Through total surrender of our wills and daily fellowship with Christ, we can realize the victorious life. But the problem persists. The basic tendencies of that old nature to rebel against God continue. The struggle is a daily challenge (Gal. 5:16-17).

"Slow to learn," "Dull of hearing," "O you of little faith." Christ worked with the problem of our sinful nature for the duration of His earthly ministry. The seriousness of our blindness is reflected in the conversation He had with Philip at the end of three and a half years of walking together. After seeing the Lord Jesus raise the dead, heal the sick, bind up the brokenhearted, and teach His entire message, Philip said, "Lord, show us the Father, and it is enough for us." Christ answered, ". . . Have I been so long with you, and yet you have not come to know me, Philip? He who has seen me has seen the Father; how can you say, 'Show us the Father?' " (John 14:8, 9). Even the Son of God had difficulty with this problem of human insensitivity.

It is not accidental that Christ stressed His long fellowship with Philip. The conversation took place the night before He died.

The father of a demon-possessed son came to Christ's disciples to be healed. He did not come to members of the crowd or to casual spectators; he came to the disciples. But they could not cure him. The Lord again dealt with the problem: "And Jesus answered and said, 'O unbelieving and perverted generation, how long shall I be with you? How long shall I put up with you? Bring him here to me' " (Matt. 17:17).

After many miracles and clear displays of His power, Christ had to admonish Peter, who was sinking after his exciting walk on the water, "O you of little faith, why did you doubt?" (Matt. 14:31).

Christ summed up the problem of our sinful nature and cautioned us concerning it in Gethsemane. "Keep watching and praying, that you may not enter into temptation; the spirit is willing, but the flesh is weak" (Matt. 26:41).

Even the disciples had a sinful nature. How could they possibly miss the majesty of Christ when they had the opportunity to see Him, touch Him, and personally witness the many miracles He performed? How could the children of Israel possibly have continued in such stubborn rebellion after the Lord opened the Red Sea for them? At every point of difficulty, whether thirst, hunger, or other misery, they complained about the Lord, moaning that He brought them into the desert to die. God gave them miracle after miracle. He rained manna from heaven, gave water from a rock, and maintained their clothes so that even their sandals did not wear out for forty years, yet they complained.

Like the disciples, we need to learn that anything short of active surrender to Christ will not suffice. Apathy, indifference, or merely doing our duty is not following his command. We must not dive into the middle of a holy huddle and turn Christianity into a self-indulgent club when the heart of our Savior reaches to those who are without. We must get away from the concept of super sainthood falsely measured by acquiring knowledge, avoiding bad habits, and keeping the clique's rules. This is not the heart of Christ. Until we are seeking those who are without Christ, we are defeated by our human nature.

Am I Sensitive to Christ?

In light of our selfish nature, it is difficult to maintain a true Christlike selflessness. It is impossible with only self-generated energy. Maintaining Christlike selflessness can be done only through the filling of the Holy Spirit which results from a life in fellowship with the Lord. In addition to warmly extending our hearts to others, we need to be aware of our vertical relationship with our Father. He has sent us, so we should conduct ourselves as His agents, loving Him and being guided by His love.

The controlling love of Christ should be the driving dynamic in the life of any spiritually healthy believer (II Cor. 5:14). This was the secret of Paul's life. The world is full of people without goals, aimlessly wandering. They seldom stop to consider, much less answer, the age-old question of why they get up in the morning. Self-seeking controls many of us, but Christ's love should drive us to pour out love to others (Rom. 5:5).

The person sensitive to his Lord and Savior then will become more and more aware that he should be seeking, should conduct himself as a sent one, should be controlled by Christ's love, and should be a conduit through whom that warm, life-changing power flows to others.

Am I Sensitive to Others?

A new believer once asked me, "How do you convince friends of their need for Christ when they have everything—money, success, a happy family, and good health?"

For a moment I hesitated, beginning the answer with Scriptures about life everlasting and the prospects for those who die without Christ. I was trying to express these truths when Christ's parable about the wealthy man came to mind. In Luke 12 Christ tells about the man whose land was very productive. The man wondered what to do with his wealth, finally concluding that he should tear down his barns and build larger ones for the surplus. His future was secure. He said to himself, "Soul, you have many goods laid up for many years to come; take your ease, eat, drink, and be merry" (Luke 12:19).

"But God said to him, 'You fool! This very night your soul is required of you; and now who will own what you have prepared?' So is the man who lays up treasure for himself, and is not rich toward God" (Luke 12:20-21).

Christians can be subtly trapped into thought patterns governed by the world's values. We should not be deceived by materialism; it dulls sensitivity to the truth of man's condition before God. Each of us at some time will come to the end of life in this body and will face a righteous God. Those without Christ face tragic futures.

Ephesians 2:12 speaks of those separated from Christ. They are strangers to the covenant of promise, "having no hope and without God in the world." We naturally tend to view our friends as good people. They are admirable citizens, acceptably carrying on their day-to-day lives. It is embarrassing to interrupt them with thoughts of God.

Are we sensitive to our friends' true condition before the Lord? Just think of it! As their lives are reviewed in judgment they are without a promise. They have no hope. They are without God. They face only eternal judgment. This truth should move the heart of every child of God to care for friends who don't know Christ.

Revelation 20:11-15 describes the final great white throne judgment of the unbelieving dead. All who are not found written in the Lamb's Book of Life will be thrown into the Lake of Fire forever. Some time ago God began to lay a particular burden for some individuals on my heart. One friend in particular kept coming into my mind. I imagined him looking over Christ's shoulder into my face asking why I had not told him. Tears were shed in prayer for many months. That friend knows Christ today.

We live and associate with people every day who do not know Jesus Christ. Many believe they are our friends. We profess to care. Yet we are not sensitive to our friends' hopeless condition without Christ. If we cared, we would tell them about the Savior. But fear of rejection, cowardice at the thought of emotional pain, and sometimes fear of embarrassment keep us from letting our friends know the way of salvation. If we truly are sensitive to their condition we should control our fears and let them know about Christ.

The Outside

Part Two deals with how to make things happen on the outside. These chapters examine New Testament passages about communicating with unbelievers and conducting ourselves wisely toward them.

This section is designed to help you break out of the holy huddle, to get close to those without Christ so they can see His love in you, understand the gospel, and as a result trust the Savior.

6

The Lifestyle
of Love

A wealthy couple decided they would go to skid row and see how the other half lived. They tried to see every facet of life, including the rescue-mission situation of those trapped in the dregs of society.

While in a meeting at the rescue mission, the couple heard the gospel. When the invitation was given they received Christ.

Because of the way they came to Christ, both developed an interest in the derelict lives of skid row. The woman began to call on people who lived there. She met one prostitute whom she encouraged to escape. The young woman made the decision and went to her wealthy friend's house.

When the prostitute appeared at the door, the maid was shocked at the "creature" standing on the front porch. The woman of the house immediately welcomed the girl, threw her arms around her, and smothered her with kisses. Having never known true love, the former prostitute collapsed under the affection.

The young woman lived for only one year after she was saved. During that time she visited houses of prostitution, detention homes, women's prisons, and other places where young women in similar circumstances might be found. By the time she went home to be with her Lord, as best anyone could calculate, she had led approximately twelve hundred people to Christ. In reviewing her life, the woman said that her gracious Christian friend had, ". . . kissed me into heaven."

In Christian Groups

Find a local church that cares for others—one that will nourish your love for others. We must be sensitive to the groups with whom we identify. In the name of Christ a great deal of legalism, hypocrisy, and hostile judgment is carried on. It breaks my heart to acknowledge this. Many believers who genuinely care for Christ and others are stopped cold in any outreach effort because of an unfortunate association with those who are frozen into an isolationist mold.

Seek out Christians with warm hearts. Those who genuinely love Christ will genuinely love others. No group is perfect. If it were perfect, it would be imperfect when I joined it! However, we can pick the best group available. Concentrate on discerning the difference between genuine sanctification and isolationism. One can live a life identified with Christ without losing contact with unbelievers. Jesus Christ did it and Paul did it. Carefully examine the groups with whom you identify.

It is easy to bask in the holy huddle's warmth. The path of least resistance is to move in reaction, not action; to drift rather than to decide as led by the Spirit of God. The conscience is seared and then salved when we let ourselves glide into a clique that approves our excessively introspective attitudes and activities. The result is total self-preoccupation.

On the other hand, the Christlike heart can be stimulated and its outreach multiplied through association with those who genuinely care for others. Great joy can be found in godly association with loving Christians whose hearts are seeking those without Christ.

The church is established of God as the pillar of truth to bear witness to Jesus Christ. We should attend local services with our families and financially support the local church. By personal example and verbal encouragement, we should urge others to become active in a Christ-honoring assembly.

The church as a local assembly is designed among other things to care for the flock. Having served in the pastorate for twelve years, I deeply sympathize with the pastor's overwhelming problems. Much of his time is consumed in caring for sick members. In the process the local church frequently becomes inward looking.

Although there are many healthy local churches with a dynamic community outreach, too often congregations follow the path of least resistance. Suffering from spiritual malnutrition and buffeted by a vicious spiritual warfare, many average church members struggle to the weekly meetings, gasping for spiritual rest and recuperation. It is easy to attend meetings and to exclude those who are outside. This happens even though the church members may say they don't approve of isolationist activity. By the very nature of human personality and the hard cruel world in which we live this inward looking life simply is the easiest path to walk.

Take a step back and look at what God has done in Christian organizations. Modern missions began with William Carey's trip to India, in spite of, rather than because of, some existing organizations. God consistently has raised up outreach organizations ranging from remote tribal translation work to next-door neighbor outreach in the American Bible Belt. Why? God wants His church to reach out. Every Christ-honoring organization is part of the invisible body of Christ, the church. Every believer should be careful in selecting his Christian organization affiliations.

Each of us should be active in and should support a local church. Each of us also should be active in obeying the Great Commission. In the lives of many Christians this takes the form of participation in and/or support of evangelistic organizations. Let your organizational lifestyle contribute to your loving outreach. Do not squelch the love of Christ through organizational activity that promotes isolationism. God will honor the life of love. God works through Christlike hearts.

In the Personal Lifestyle

If the love of Christ truly controls, then it must begin to show up in personal lifestyle. With whom do you have lunch? With whom do you participate in your favorite sport or hobby? Whom do you have in your home for dinner, refreshments, or casual social contact? Your lifestyle must be conceived in love. It must continue in love. If love controls you, then you will spend time with unbelievers.

Paul explains his method of finding common ground with those who do not know Christ. The classic "all things to all men" passage is effectively paraphrased by the Living New Testament. "Yes, whatever a person is like, I try to find common ground with him so that he will let me tell him about Christ and let Christ save him" (I Cor. 9:22b).

What is common ground and how do you find it? Common ground certainly is not superficially liking "the same things." If you like yellow and I like yellow that does not in and of itself give us common ground. Common ground has more to do with the basic attitudes of life. It deals with real priorities, desires, and values. Love creates common ground. We all need love and we respond to those who genuinely offer it.

How can love be offered? Begin to spend time with people. Do what they like to do and what you like to do. Everyone must eat; perhaps you could begin by having lunch together. Do not wait for an opportunity to pounce on your friend with the gospel. Listen carefully. Find out what is important to that person. Let him know he is important to you. Soon you will receive a positive response.

Count on God to Help

"Unless the Lord builds the house, we labor in vain" (Ps. 127:1a). Only the Lord can deliver hopeless prisoners from Satan's slavery, but Christ's plan for this includes children who obey His instructions. For example, Christ has commanded us to pray for those who do not know Christ, with the assurance that He desires all men to be saved and come to the knowledge of the truth (I Tim. 2:1-4). Christ is not willing for any to perish (II Peter 3:9). Furthermore, He sees that all things work together for good to those who love God, to those who are called according to His purpose (Rom. 8:28). Christ has ordered that we should actively produce good works (Eph. 2:10). In Christ's lovingkindness He will teach us the way in which we should go, counseling with His eye on us (Ps. 32:8). If we trust in Christ with all our heart, He will guide us in His ways (Prov. 3:5-6).

How does this apply to the seeking lifestyle of love? God loves those who are lost. Christ died for them. He wants to reach them through us. If we live the biblical principles of love, God will be at work opening doors (Col. 4:3), guiding us to those whose hearts He has prepared. This is one of the secrets for defeating fear. In this Christlike lifestyle you will find that God is mightily at work in your life. Like everything else, this process of making friends and leading them to Christ takes time, but you can count on the Lord to lead you to hearts He has touched.

It is easy to sit and think of all the reasons why we can never reach others. And we never will be unless God is at work. The point of Scripture is that God has committed Himself to work and guide the Christian to those who do not know Him, so that they can have life everlasting. The only way we can experience God's mighty power is to give it a try. Begin to share your personal life with those who do not know Christ. They have been rejected long enough.

7

It Happens
Outside the Formula

We had come to the third meeting of a New Life discussion series.[1] We were involved in the details of a guest prayer list. In addition, we were establishing a prayer chain for one week immediately preceding the first guest participation night.

A couple without Christ unexpectedly came to this session. They had heard about it and wanted to get involved. My heart sank. They sat right next to me as the Christians began to discuss their non-Christian friends and how we should pray for them. The believers did not know who these people were and proceeded as if they were members of

1. New Life carries on a discussion series of seven sessions which are designed to reach those who do not know Christ. These meetings are divided into two sections. The first three are for believers who meet together to pray, plan, and learn how to discuss Christ with friends in a loving way. The guests do not attend until the fourth meeting, which is the first of the four discussion sessions.

the family. One of the Christians, as we were getting volunteers to pray every thirty minutes around the clock, observed, "Man, those non-Christians don't have a chance. We're going to pray them right into heaven." At that point I was wishing I could disappear. But God was at work.

When the meeting was over the non-Christian man lit a cigarette, took a puff, and said to me, "Matt, we have got to get together." When I asked him why, he stated that he was scared to death—scared because he now realized he should not go into eternity without Christ. The next morning we got together and he prayed to receive Christ. Since then he has been active as a child of God, growing in the faith and letting others know about the Savior.

What happened? Our neat formula was ignored. Our plan was to have three meetings for Christians to be followed by four discussion sessions for unbelievers. The whole order had been shockingly disrupted by this unbeliever's attendance at a session for insiders only, yet the biblical principles were at work. We loved him and he knew it. We had been sharing our lives with him, and he could sense all of the ingredients from urgency to affirmation in our hearts for him. The point is vital. When the biblical principles of friendship evangelism are followed, God Almighty will be at work through our lives, touching those without Him, even if our human plans are not followed in every detail.

Begin in Heartfelt Prayer

Colossians 4:2-6 is one of the major biblical passages detailing God's principles for relating to those without Christ. It has a lot to say about how to pray: "Devote yourselves to prayer, keeping alert in it with an attitude of thanksgiving."

Most of us devote ourselves to *ourselves* in prayer. We pray for our families, our churches, our pastors, and others in God's work. How many believers devote prayer time to unbelievers?

An old truth about goal setting is: no target, no hit. If we do not set objectives, then we certainly will not reach them. This is true in our prayer lives. If we believe God, then we will be praying for those in whom He is interested. If we really love those without Christ, and if we genuinely want to give ourselves to them so that they can have Jesus Christ, then we will find ourselves devoting a great part of our private lives to them. Review your Christian life. Have you really devoted yourself to a non-Christian in prayer?

This passage was the text for one of the happier occasions in my life. I was speaking to the students at a well-known seminary. After the message, one student wanted to talk. He was a mature man who had gone from a successful career to the seminary in answer to God's call on his life. He affirmed that he was very devoted to Jesus Christ. However, he admitted that he never had been devoted to a non-Christian in prayer.

God answers prayer. Do we avail ourselves of prayer's immense potential? Each of us can thrill at what we have seen God do in our lives in answer to prayer. Outreach to non-Christians is no different than any other vital part of the Christian life. It must begin in prayer. Unless God works, we labor in vain. We must rely on Him, which most often should begin with much intercessory work before His throne for the lost for whom He died.

Colossians 4:2 admonishes us to keep alert with an attitude of thanksgiving. Do you ever catch yourself mumbling, thoughtlessly repeating tired cliches in prayer? All too frequently I find myself praying for three or four minutes without the slightest idea of what I have just said. The old cliches keep coming around: " . . . guide, bless, and direct," " . . . dear precious heavenly Father," " . . . guide, bless, and direct . . . ," " . . . dear precious heavenly Father."

Do we really have our spiritual armor polished, sharpened, and ready to go to war for those who are without Christ before the throne of God? When we get on our knees filthy thoughts, mental blanks, and ludicrous distractions can keep us from the main business. Here is where a lot of the spiritual warfare is won or lost. The solution comes about through alert prayer, mindful of the desperate condition of those without Christ.

Ask God to Open Doors

The mighty apostle Paul, probably the greatest living Christian of his day, had a great need. He asks that his brothers and sisters pray for an open door. " . . . praying at the same time for us as well, that God may open up to us a door for the word, so that we may speak forth the mystery of Christ, for which I have also been imprisoned; . . . " (Col. 4:3).

The seemingly impenetrable defenses of the non-Christian can be discouraging. In their spiritual darkness they do not understand the gospel. Furthermore, they do not seem interested in anything we have to say about the Savior. We see their glazed fixation on our left earlobe. We know we've lost them. Nothing is more devastating than being ignored.

One of the secrets for penetrating that spiritual indifference is united prayer for open doors. When Christians band together to pray, God miraculously goes to work. It happens in a variety of ways with dependable consistency. One dramatic episode I had was with a man whom I dearly loved, but who simply could not understand the gospel.

This man lived in another town, and I was spending about two hours a week with him. Our time together was rapidly drawing to a close. Nothing I said moved him toward Christ. I tried reverse psychology. I tried fancy footwork and clever moves. My friend was impervious. Many of my Christian friends in the nucleus were praying for him.

During our next to last session, the sense of urgency was immense. Realizing that everything attempted had failed, I began to pray earnestly as instructed in Colossians 4:3. I asked God to open a door, confessing that everything I had tried had been to no avail. As far as I knew, I was not operating with my own energy, but in complete dependence on the Lord. Everything I knew about reaching the unreached had been tried and was not working. I told the Lord that I had used all my resources. Unless He opened the door, nothing would happen.

While I was praying I became aware that the man was talking. He was driving his car and I was sitting beside him in the front seat. I began to listen and heard him say, "Matt, I'd like to be sure Christ is my personal Savior, but I just don't know how." Immediately my heart leaped Godward with a quick prayer of thanksgiving: "Thank you, Lord; I believe the door is open now." Within forty-five minutes my friend received Christ as his Savior.

That was several years ago. The man continues in fellowship with and service for Jesus Christ. Many Christians were praying for the open door and I was praying desperately for the open door. God opened the door.

Perhaps you have been discouraged because nothing has happened in your efforts to reach others. Follow the biblical principles of prayer. Get several friends to join you in praying that a specific door will open. God never tells us to do something that He will not enable us to do. God never tells us to pray about things, intending to frustrate us. He answers prayer.

Pray to Make it Clear

In Paul's continuing plea for prayer, he makes an unusual request—one that astounds me: " . . . in order that I may make it clear in the way I ought to speak" (Col. 4:4). Can you imagine that? The mighty apostle Paul wanted the average Christians at Colossae to pray that he would make the gospel clear. Of all people, Paul knew the gospel and could make it clear. Before this letter was written, he wrote the Epistle to the Romans, which makes the gospel as clear as any document. Yet he insists on asking for prayer that he make the gospel clear. Why?

Paul faced the reality that non-Christians do not understand the gospel. We consistently get into trouble by assuming otherwise.

How many times have you heard people say that a certain unbelieving friend has been raised in the church and has been around gospel preaching all of his life? They say that he knows the Bible just as well as we do, that he understands the gospel, that he could preach the gospel. In the overwhelming majority of cases, that simply is not true. People refuse to talk about the gospel, acting like they understand it. What they understand is not the gospel but some false gospel.

Once an individual in a New Life discussion said, "I know all about your gospel and don't want a thing to do with it." I asked him for an explanation of the gospel. (It is never right to put words in another's mouth. Good communication requires care that we are using terms with common definitions.) It took a few minutes of diplomatic pressing for a definition, but eventually I got it: "Unless you suffer and are poor, Jesus will not save you"!

On another occasion, I spent over sixteen months trying to explain the gospel to a man. Finally we came to the moment of truth. He sat still long enough for me to go through all of the details with him. He responded affirmatively to each essential ingredient as set forth in Chapter 3. At the end of our conversation, he indicated that he was ready to do whatever it took to be a Christian.

At this point, I began to illustrate what John 1:12 (receiving Christ) meant. I used the illustration of a Christmas present to tell the man that salvation is a gift. Finally I asked him how one receives the gift of eternal life. He looked up at me, shrugged his shoulders, and said, "Do something good." It took another thirty minutes of detailed explanation to be sure he understood the gospel. Then he prayed to receive Christ.

Never assume that an unbeliever understands the gospel. He does not. Get Christians to band together in prayer that the gospel will be made clear to the individual involved.

Wisdom

Many Christians are made to feel guilty if they are not rudely invading other lives. There seems to be some unwritten rule that unless we embarrass ourselves or in some way display colossally bad manners, then we have not stood our ground for Christ. This is not scriptural. The Bible teaches that God's way is the wise way. "Conduct yourselves with wisdom toward outsiders. . ." (Col. 4:5a).

What is the wisest possible course to follow in a relationship with an unbeliever?

Listen to your friend. Be sensitive to who he is, what he is, and where he is. Then ask God to guide you in relating to him. What you do will vary with each individual. Find common ground. Let him know you are with him. He will sense your genuine love. Then look for the wisest way to let him know about Christ.

A young couple came to Christ through the New Life work. I considered them my grandchildren in the faith. My spiritual grandson came to me with the proposition that we should attempt to reach his business partner for Christ. This was to be his first project in witnessing. I knew his partner to be a defensive, hostile individual. I recommended that a more receptive person first be approached. But my "grandson" persisted. He already had set up a dinner meeting.

Anticipating what might be encountered, I tried to teach my friend something about spiritual realities. I told him that I would gladly come on one condition—that we did not discuss the Lord. He looked devastated. No doubt my image was crumbling before his eyes, but I had good reasons for this request. His partner would come with strong defenses, daring us to talk about God. If we tried to meet him head on, a fight was inevitable. We would never win him that way. I suggested that we simply spend a pleasant evening together, and make the business partner beg if he wanted to talk about spiritual matters. My friend reluctantly agreed.

The momentous evening came. My new Christian friend's wife attended the dinner also. She was a sensitive woman, rejoicing in her new found life in Christ. The unbelieving business partner took nefarious pleasure in needling her that evening. We had not been seated more than ten minutes when he said, with a sideways glance at his hostess, "If there is a God, he shouldn't be mad at me. I've never done anything wrong."

My response was, "That's interesting. Do you play the guitar?" He said no. I then asked about his hobbies and he told me about them in detail.

Soon he repeated his point that if there was a God, he should not be mad at him, since he was innocent of any wrongdoing. My response again was that that was very interesting and would he please tell me about the new business ventures he and his partner were in.

In one form or another, this went on throughout the evening. The guest would try to bring up the subject of God in an argumentative way. I refused to respond in kind.

This conversational pattern continued until fifteen minutes before it was time to leave. I then asked our friend if I could ask him a personal question, to which he responded yes. So I asked, "Are you some kind of religious fanatic?"

"No. Why did you ask me that?"

"Well, you've been trying to talk about God all night. I just thought you might be one of those religious fanatics."

He got the point. He could sense that we were Christians and cared about him but did not want to argue. He asked if we could get together again. I let him know that I would like to pursue the friendship. We did.

We began to have lunch together about once a month. Each time he would try to argue about evolution and biblical creation or some such subject. Each time I would refuse to argue. After one lunch he said, "Can we get together again sometime?" I assured him that we certainly could, but why? "Because if it really is heaven or hell, I want to be sure I get it right."

The time had come. I told him that at last he had struck on a subject concerning which I was an expert. I could let him know everything he needed to know about going to heaven. If he wanted, I could help him be sure he was God's child forever.

There is a sequel to the story. My grandson and granddaughter and others in the faith surrounded this man with love. He grew in the faith. Later on his elderly father-in-law trusted Christ. Then his mother-in-law came to the Savior.

What wisdom calls for will vary from person to person. Some people are hungry for the Lord and are almost immediately receptive. The wisest course in these cases is a direct approach to the gospel. In other cases the prudent path is to hang back, waiting for the opportune time.

Make the Most of Godly Opportunity

Immediately following the instruction about wisdom is the exhortation in Colossians 4:5 about ". . . making the most of the opportunity." This requires maintaining a proper balance in personal relationships so we can allow the opportunity to lead the person to Christ to arise and recognize it when it comes. Admittedly, the tightrope walk of Christian balance is difficult.

Some Christians have things under control. They are wise. They never get ruffled. They never offend people. They are so cool that they never lead anybody to Christ. We must avoid being so "wise" that we maneuver ourselves into total inactivity. We must make the most of the opportunity.

How can we make the most of the opportunity? Begin with a compliment and make an effort to close the transaction with a biblical invitation to receive Christ as Savior, as detailed in Chapter 3. The Holy Spirit will guide you in each case. However, you should be alert to the differing situations and ways of introducing people to Him.

Once the person is assured that you respect him and appreciate his interest, the stage is set for the opportunity to invite him to receive Christ. Be ready to move on to your presentation of the gospel, followed immediately by an invitation for that individual to receive Christ as Savior. Be spiritually alert, ready to make the most of any opportunity when it is there.

8

Tailor-Made Words

The daughter of a fashionable couple from a large eastern city went to Africa as a Peace Corps volunteer. She had been to finishing school and her parents had made every effort to see that she was properly prepared to occupy a place in their social strata.

When the young woman's term on the field was over she sent a telegram announcing that she would be bringing her new husband home with her. Her mother and father waited with excited anticipation at the airport gate. Their daughter emerged from the plane on the arm of a man about seven feet tall who was adorned in feathers, beads, skulls, tigers' teeth, and assorted pouches of magical potions around his neck. He even had a bone through his nose and rings in his ears. The mother fainted. As the father held his now unconscious wife, he shouted to his daughter, "No, no, dear. We said a *rich* doctor."

Even in the closest of families communications sometimes are not clear. The Christian needs to be specially sensitive to what people say and how they hear. We, above all people, should be aware of the fact that most communications are nonverbal. We must also realize that people do not always mean what they say.

Responding to People, Not Words

In concluding his instructions about our wisdom walk toward outsiders, Paul says, "Let your speech always be with grace, seasoned, as it were with salt, so that you may know how you should respond to each person" (Col. 4:6).

Our speech is to be tailored for each person. This is not only wise; it is good manners. Tailored speech is based on a presupposition that we have listened enough to know who that person is and where he is. If people know we are genuinely interested in them, it will not be too long before they will begin to let us know their innermost thoughts. We need to patiently listen. Paul instructs us to respond to the person, not to his words.

God does not intend for us to throw up verbal stumbling blocks. If a particular word is offensive to a non-Christian friend, look for ways of communicating the same truth with other language.

A friend once repeatedly came to see me, obviously interested not only in doing business, but in understanding what Christians were all about. After a year it seemed to me the time for winning him was right. I invited him to lunch.

He immediately became defensive, saying, "Now, Matt, I am a Christian." I knew he had been raised in a particular denomination and was very concerned that I accept him as a religious person. I therefore acknowledged that he was a

Christian, adding that I knew of his denominational background. He was relieved.

Then I said, "I did not want to talk to you about that." He was appreciative and willing to enter into any conversation I wanted. I asked him if he knew what would happen when he died, and he said no. I told him that this is what we should talk about. He agreed. One hour later he trusted Christ as his Savior.

An argument easily could have started over the definition of "Christian." We could still be arguing about the distinction between organizational membership, institutionalization, and New Testament regeneration. Rather than argue, however, I preferred to accept his definition and respond where he was. He wanted to know the Lord, yet needed to be reaffirmed as a good person who was doing his best in the religion he knew. Therefore, the choice was made to avoid the emotional conflict and rather to meet his sincere desire to know the Lord. Without compromise he came to Christ. He now knows what a real Christian is.

Communicating with Wisdom

The New Testament commands us not to be quarrelsome, but to be kind, able to teach, and able to gently correct those who are in opposition. The following passage gives helpful detailed instruction about communicating with unbelievers.

And the Lord's bond-servant must not be quarrelsome, but be kind to all, able to teach, patient when wronged, with gentleness correcting those who are in opposition, if perhaps God may grant them repentance leading to the knowledge of the truth, and they may come to their senses and escape from the snare of the devil, having been held captive by him to do his will (Tim. 2:24-26).

"The Lord's bond-servant must not be quarrelsome" (24a).

How much that goes on in the name of witnessing is nothing more than a fight? Much of our clannish structured Christianity trains us to be insecure and defensive. Somehow our old nature combines with some part of these insecurities to make us ready for a fight. And sometimes perhaps the old nature does it alone, even in the believer who is secure in his faith. In any event, we find ourselves quick to quarrel over the dependability of the Bible and over other key questions of the faith.

It is sometimes difficult to avoid arguments with pressing unbelievers, so we must use wisdom and respond quietly out of love. If we genuinely love people, then we will not be quarrelsome. We will be concerned for their well-being.

"Be kind to all, able to teach, patient when wronged" (24b).

The old law of sowing and reaping has no more profound application than in the area of human relationships. Kindness produces a crop of its own. When we are kind to people, they are willing to listen to us. If, on the other hand, we are judgmental, rejecting them, they will be inclined to respond accordingly.

We should be able to teach. There is no spiritual premium on ignorance. In this same chapter Paul encouraged Timothy to be diligent in pursuing the Word of Truth (v. 15). Paul listed knowledge as one of his major weapons in the spiritual warfare (II Cor. 6:6-7). Bible study is essential to equipping our gift for service (II Tim. 3:16-17).

Verse 24 also gives an important caveat: be patient when wronged. Count on being wronged at times in your witness. A natural reaction is to withdraw, but forewarned should mean forearmed. Expect to be wronged and, in the love of Christ, be prepared to patiently endure. This is one of the hardest things to do. Patient endurance is a fruit of the Spirit, and He will enable us to do it (Gal. 5:22-23). This kind of interpersonal relationship will make its own impact for Christ.

"With gentleness correcting those who are in opposition" (25a).

Correction is one of the most vital and difficult instructions for witnessing. How can we gently correct those who are in opposition? So much human emotion is involved that the task seems almost impossible. However, it can be done.

The most successful approach I have found is to avoid any me-versus-you confrontation with the unbeliever. It is not you against the unbeliever. When it comes to religious opinions, it is the unbeliever versus Christ.

The early believers followed a winning pattern. They consistently gave witness to Christ's resurrection. It is helpful to remember that the non-Christian has never squarely faced the issue.

Either Jesus Christ came out of the grave or He did not. If He did—and the evidence is overwhelming that He did— then we have a Savior who conquered death itself and who has the answers for all of us. Therefore, one of the first things we can do in gently correcting the unbeliever is to keep lovingly reminding him of the real question: Did Jesus Christ come out of the grave, or not? If He did, then it is not an issue of my opinion versus yours.

This agreement on the question gives an opportunity for a pleasant exchange. You can insist on your friend's right to have his own opinion. As a witness of Jesus Christ all you are doing is humbly suggesting that he consider the credentials of this majestic individual who entered the human race over nineteen hundred years ago. Then consider Christ and His opinions and lovingly ask if it isn't really your friend against Christ.

A man was extremely defensive in a New Life discussion. He asked if reincarnation were a possibility. My answer was that reincarnation certainly is a possibility—if Jesus Christ is not who He says He is. The man was disarmed because I was not fighting with him. I then used that situation to introduce another means of gentle correction.

I admitted that I could be wrong. How refreshing for a non-Christian to hear this from a Christian! You and I know Jesus Christ and believe with all of our hearts that we are right. But speaking to the non-Christian from what he can know as a natural man without Christ, I can admit that from the natural man's position I could be wrong. My point of gentle correction is that my friend should consider Jesus Christ. If Christ is right, then the unbeliever is wrong and should change his mind, receiving Christ. The unbeliever has far more to lose if he is in error.

That man who brought up the subject of reincarnation was willing to reconsider. Reincarnation was not a big point to him. He was only using it to argue. After several other attempts to quarrel, he eventually prayed with me to receive Christ. Within a year and a half more than a score of his friends had trusted the Savior. He later told his wife that he had tried every way he could to fight, and, if I would have responded in kind, he would never have come back or considered Christ again. He didn't succeed in fighting. He sensed love, was gently corrected, and received the Savior.

Let me summarize. Try to put yourself in the position of the unbeliever who sees Christians as bullheaded, blind clansmen fighting for their narrow-minded position. That potentially hostile situation can be controlled by the simple admission that we could be wrong. Here are the logical steps for gently correcting: (1) I admit that I could be wrong. If Jesus Christ ever fails to be who He claims to be then I am wrong. (2) Consider Jesus Christ. Your opinion is just as good as mine. This is not me against you. It is you against Christ. (3) Did Christ conquer the grave, or didn't He? If He did, then He is right, and you are wrong. (4) If we do not trust Christ, where is our hope? There is no answer without Him.

"They may come to their senses" (25b-26).

God's pattern is that once this immensely demanding approach has been taken, the unbeliever might repent, come to his senses, and escape from the snare of the devil. Notice the Scriptural pattern. The unbeliever is not argued into the kingdom of heaven. He is not bludgeoned to repentance. He comes to his own senses. This is the happy result of loving, gentle correction.

Listen from a Caring Heart

In one of his more classic passages Paul describes the Christian life as an athletic contest, detailing his determined efforts to serve the Lord.

> Do you not know that those who run in a race all run, but only one receives the prize? Run in such a way that you

may win. And everyone who competes in the games exercises self-control in all things. They then do it to receive a perishable wreath, but we an imperishable. Therefore I run in such a way, as not without aim; I box in such a way, as not beating the air; but I buffet my body and make it my slave, lest possibly, after I have preached to others, I myself should be disqualified (I Cor. 9:24-27).

This passage is relatively familiar. The context is not. What is Paul talking about? He is talking about winning others to Jesus Christ. His guiding principle is: "I have become all things to all men, that I may by all means save some" (I Cor. 9:22b). Or as the Living Bible paraphrases: "Yes, whatever a person is like, I try to find common ground with him so he will let me tell him about Christ and let Christ save him." Paul knew that common ground is the best way to win people to Jesus Christ. If we lovingly spend time genuinely seeking to know others, to listen patiently, then one day—perhaps sooner than we think—they find that we share some values and goals. In the early stages this requires more listening than talking.

Usually this discovery happens almost imperceptibly. People have basic emotional needs. They face common frustrations, joys, rewards, and disappointments. By listening from a caring heart, we soon find what their real values are. Most individuals want others to know their desires and deep feelings about life's important issues. Once we demonstrate genuine concern, hear them out, and respond to their words lovingly, we have developed a receptivity to our message.

9

Breaking Out
of the Holy Huddle

It took five years for a loyal friend to come to Christ. He was hostile toward Bible thumpers and the hellfire and brimstone approach. In his experience Christian witnessing was full of negatives.

This man was a client during my years of law practice. Through many difficult times I stood by him, sometimes when he could not pay. If business did not call for being together, I would arrange a lunch to keep close personal contact. After five years, he let me tell him about the Savior, about life everlasting, about life in all of its fullness now. He agreed with me that there was a hell to be avoided and he trusted Christ.

Why would he listen to me and not to the "hellfire and brimstone preachers" about whom he constantly complained? He kept repeating "Matt, we are friends, and I feel like I can talk to you." Over the years I had demonstrated my friendship beyond a reasonable doubt.

Contact Work

It is God's will that we share our lives with those who do not know Christ. God's method always has been that His child should go with His message to someone without Him.

One of the most vital keys to successful New Testament friendship evangelism is the secret of relaxing with unbelieving friends. Those who are without Christ will respond to affirming Christians. Time must be spent in direct contact with unbelievers. If your life is failing to touch lives without Him, measure it by this question: "Am I in meaningful, continuing contact with someone without Christ?" It is at this point where many Christians falter.

Why is contact work so successful? Because we spend time with the people we like. People appreciate being around others who are receptive and care for the little details as well as the big issues in their lives. Friends without Christ can best see our real love through personal contact.

We are in great danger of becoming a religion of words and studies. We continue to learn, hiding God's Word in our notebooks so that we may have bigger notebooks. Instead, Christ's truth should find expression in daily life. The enemy and our own deceitful hearts have subtly turned us from the biblical way of lovingly spending time with unbelievers. The Bible analyzes this important facet in several ways.

Shine in Darkness, Not in Light

You are the light of the world. A city set on a hill cannot be hidden. Nor do men light a lamp, and put it under the peck-measure, but on the lampstand; and it gives light to all who are in the house. Let your light shine before men in such a way that they may see your good works, and glorify your Father who is in heaven (Matt. 5:14-16).

Christ said that we are to shine in the darkness, not always in the light. Those without Him are to see that beautiful glow He brings into His children's lives. Are we shining where people can see us? Or are we happy to just meet in the holy huddle and shine all over each other?

I don't mean to minimize the importance of shining on each other. Each gift is to be used in the body to help others. We are to nurture and care for one another. It is urgent, however, that we shine before unbelievers. This is what most Christians are unwilling to do.

Do all things without grumbling or disputing; that you may prove yourselves to be blameless and innocent, children of God above reproach in the midst of a crooked and perverse generation, among whom you appear as lights in the world, holding fast the word of life, so that in the day of Christ I may have cause to glory because I did not run in vain nor toil in vain (Phil. 2:14-16).

Paul repeated Christ's teaching. In a crooked and perverse world we are to shine as lights, holding forth the Word of Life. Unbelievers are agonizing under the awful anxieties of life, plunging through darkness toward the precipice of eternity. Left to their own devices, they are incapable of freeing themselves from evil's slavery. Unbelievers cannot see Christ in their darkness. They will not come to us. God has commanded us to go to them.

The point of the scriptural admonition is that we get out in the middle of that stream of unenlightened humanity and let them see the light of God in our lives. One of the beautiful announcements of Christ's coming was that God's tender mercy had appeared, and with it the sunrise to shine on those who sit in darkness and in the shadow of death, to guide our feet into the way of peace (Luke 1:78-79).

Sensitive Christians can repeatedly hear others say that they never would have known Christ unless someone had cared enough to come into their lives to communicate His Good News. One man told me that he had been involved in religious activities all his life. His question was: "How could I possibly have sat through religious service after religious service without receiving Christ?"

Christ's Contact with Unbelievers

Now all the tax-gatherers and the sinners were coming near Him to listen to Him. And both the Pharisees and the scribes began to grumble, saying, "This man receives sinners and eats with them" (Luke 15:1-2).

And when the Pharisees saw this, they said to His disciples, "Why does your Teacher eat with the tax-gatherers and sinners?" (Matt. 9:11).

These reports describe part of Christ's practice of spending a lot of time in direct contact with needy unbelievers. He did not speak *at* them. He cared for them. He ate and drank with them.

Luke 5 gives a touching account of the calling of the first disciples, of some early miracles, and of the feast Matthew prepared for Christ in his home.

Christ found Peter and Andrew, James and John at the lakeside and went with them into their boat. He took part in their everyday lives. Great changes began right there.

Immediately after the call of those four, Christ met a leper. With loving compassion Christ touched him and freed him from the hopeless misery of his disease. Christ then made Himself available to people in a home. While He was teaching, four men lowered a man through the roof. Christ forgave the sinner and made him well. Then He went to the reception in Levi's home.

Christ moved among the people. He taught, He discipled, He worked with individuals and with groups, He healed, He encouraged, He warned, and He ministered to people's needs.

The four Gospels record at least 132 such contacts with people. Ten of these were in the temple and in synagogues. The other 122 were with people where they lived.

Christ spent most of His life being available to those who needed Him. We should spend most of our lives in contact with those who need Him.

If we follow Christ's example, we will break out of the holy huddle.

Paul's Contact with Unbelievers

"Having thus a fond affection for you, we were well pleased to impart to you not only the Gospel of God but also our own lives, because you had become very dear to us" (I Thess. 2:8). When Paul, the mighty apostle to the Gentiles, visited cities, dynamic impact was made for Christ. Paul was greatly empowered with apostolic gifts, signs, and miracle-working powers. In addition, however, much of his power came from sharing himself with those who did not know the Savior.

Paul's last meeting with the Ephesian elders is one of the most touching events in the New Testament. He began his conversation by reaffirming that from his first day in Asia, he was with them the whole time (Acts 20:18). He went on to say that his teaching was both public and from house to house (v. 20). Paul had affection for others and was willing to share not only a message but his life.

God's Method

"For God, who said, 'Light shall shine out of darkness,' is the One who has shone in our hearts to give the light of the knowledge of the glory of God in the face of Christ" (II Cor. 4:6). God's method is for unbelievers to see Christ in our hearts, not in our intellects. They will not see Him in our brilliant ability to out-argue them, but in our hearts.

Paul's autobiographical sketch emphasized that he presented the unadulterated truth of God. He had nothing to do with craftiness or contaminating the Word of God (II Cor. 4:2). He immediately explained the darkened condition of those who are perishing. The God of this world has blinded the minds of the unbelieving so they cannot see the light of the gospel (II Cor. 4:3-4).

How then can someone without Christ, blinded by the cunning enemy of our souls and all of his darkened forces, ever see Jesus Christ? God's plan centers in the loving believer. He lives in us. We are the light of the world. We are to shine in the darkness, but we have to get close enough so the unbeliever can see.

Verse 5 of this passage stresses that we concentrate on Christ, not on ourselves. We serve for Jesus' sake, rather than trying to make people followers of our assorted cliques.

The consummating truths are in verses 6 and 7. God lives in every Christian. It is not egotistical to believe that we are God's gift to the world. It is His stated truth.

Verse 7 adds a caution. The treasure is in very fragile vessels. We must rely on God, not on our own strength. Nothing will happen unless He works. No clever devices or human formulae can pierce the satanic darkness. Only God, shining through frail vessels, can do that. So the frail vessels need to be close enough for the unbeliever to see, not huddled together, casting their glow inward, using their very fraility as an excuse for failing to shine outwardly.

Try an Experiment

How do you begin to make contact with unbelieving friends? Try an experiment. First, pick your six best prospects. Set aside two hours a week for contact time. Have lunch, go bowling, play tennis, just visit, but do something with each one about once every three weeks. Spend an hour each with the first two this week, an hour each with the next two the next week, and so on. Every third week you will be spending one hour with one of these friends.

If the individual wants to know why you are doing this, just speak the truth in terms he or she can understand. Tell the person that, in an increasingly impersonal world, you refuse to be too preoccupied to make friends. You have decided to spend time with people who are important to you. Then listen.

You may find yourself getting together more frequently with those who are receptive. After a while, they will bring up a subject that will give you the open door. You can then honestly recognize their genuine interest and get into the gospel.

Some Christians become terrified at the thought of "witnessing." Let me suggest that you begin your contact work by resolving not to bring up the subject at all. Only respond to any spiritual suggestions the other person may bring up. Be reluctant. They will sense that you genuinely care for them and are not out to push a particular brand of religion.

Once that affirming relationship is established, the bridge of friendship can be built.

It is important that you take the pressure off yourself. Instead, pray for these people, and expect God to work in their hearts. Come to them as a loving, receptive person. Before you know it, they will show an interest in Christ.

10

Winning May Not Be Everything but It's What God Wants

Perhaps you have heard about the woman who told her neighbor that the reports about smoking and cancer had her so alarmed that she simply had to give up reading.

And so it goes with many Christians. When the moment of truth comes that the child of God must face the Great Commission, frequently he or she "gives up reading." This is in direct contrast to what pleases God. God called David a man after His own heart. That rugged hero of the faith thirsted for and obeyed God's Word (Ps. 119:16, 47, 48, 105, 106, 112, 129, 131). We also should obey. Obedience includes positive effort to win others. This requires direct action.

Extend an Invitation

If you want a friend to come to your home for dinner, you extend an invitation. This is common courtesy. If you have something good you want to share, you invite someone to join you. One of the problems with our legalistic clansmanship is that we have made it almost impossible to follow the biblical approach of inviting friends to receive the Savior. We have made them the enemy rather than victims of the enemy. The biblical norm is that our hearts be filled with love for Christ and for those who are lost, witnessing to the great blessings we have received from Christ, then inviting our friends to receive the Savior.

Some years ago a man was visiting an attorney in his office. As the visitor started to leave he turned to the attorney and said, "By the way, Scofield, are you a Christian?" The lawyer answered that he was not, in response to which the Christian asked, "Why aren't you?" "Because no one has ever invited me," Scofield answered. The man asked if he would like to be invited. The enthusiastic response was yes. The thoughtful believer then lovingly invited him to receive the Lord Jesus Christ as his Savior.

Scofield, as you may know, was the well-known C. I. Scofield who later edited the reference Bible which has been a source of profound help to many. Scofield told this story often to demonstrate the importance of extending the invitation.

Christ Invited People

Come to me, all who are weary and heavy laden, and I will give you rest. Take my yoke upon you, and learn from me, for I am gentle and humble in heart; and you shall find rest for your souls. For my yoke is easy, and my load is light (Matt. 11:28-30).

The invitation could not be more lovingly, clearly, or concisely stated: "Come to me. . . ." Christ promised rest for the weary and heavy laden. How long has it been since you invited someone to come to Christ?

In addition to personally extending the invitation, Christ instructed His disciples to go into the harvest fields (John 4:35-38). He sent them out to reap, not to make observations or to simply sow seed. The context of this passage strengthens the imperative of the Great Commission to harvest. In John 4:34, Christ said that His food was to do the will of the Father who had sent Him and to accomplish His work. The next thing Christ said is that the fields are white for harvest. He admonished the disciples to lift up their eyes and look at the fields. Are we so excessively introspective today in evaluating the various evangelistic methods that we do not see the fields ready for harvest?

Christ's harvest theology was reflected in His call to Peter and Andrew. Putting it in terms fishermen could understand, He said, "Follow me, and I will make you become fishers of men" (Mark 1:17), and again, "Do not fear, from now on you will be catching men" (Luke 5:10b).

Instead of pursuing so many cop-outs conveniently available for our basic reluctance to do Christ's will, we should have open hearts to what He teaches. We should take positive action that will continue until the lost are saved.

Paul Fought to Win People

"To the weak I became weak, that I might win the weak; I have become all things to all men, that I may by all means save some" (I Cor. 9:22). During the extended explanation of his ministry to the church at Corinth, Paul described his beliefs, attitudes, and methods for reaching the unsaved. The famous "all things to all men" passage concludes with the analogy of the dedicated athlete (I Cor. 9:26-27). Why did Paul run so certainly, box with such determination, and discipline his body with such vigor? To win people to Jesus Christ. Paul didn't stop until they were saved. In verse 19 Paul commits himself to slavery for all "that I might win the more." He then goes on five times to make the statement between verses 19 and 22 that his goal is to "win" people to Christ. There is little question among the Greek scholars that the word Paul uses for "win" is used in the missionary context.

Paul speaks again of appearing before the judgment seat of Christ. With this in view, he worked all the harder to persuade men, to win them to Christ (II Cor. 5:11). His sense of urgency was intense. He begged men to be reconciled to God (II Cor. 5:20).

Peter Pressed for Decisions

Peter's historic Pentecost message, delivered shortly after the resurrection of Christ, presses for decisions. "Repent. Be saved from this perverse generation!" Three thousand believers were added to the church that day (Acts 2:41).

John Extended the Invitation

John said that he wrote his gospel account so that the reader might believe that Jesus is the Christ, the Son of God, and that by believing he might have life in His name (John 20:30-31).

Our Lord used this mighty apostle to conclude the New Testament and the Bible. Some have observed that God used Peter to start the church, Paul to develop it, and John to complete it. John was with Christ from the beginning, observed the birth and growth of the church, outlived Paul by approximately the same amount of time that Paul had outlived Christ, and while on Patmos was inspired by God to write the Book of Revelation.

With a heart full of loving urgency, John wrote that the day would come in eternity when the one who was wrong would still be wrong, the one who was filthy would still be filthy, and the one who was righteous would still be righteous. Today is the day of grace; anyone can still be saved as long as he lives on earth. But the time will come when the day of salvation will be past. Against this background John extends the invitation to every thirsty human being to come to the Lord Jesus Christ.

"And the Spirit and the bride say, 'Come.' And let the one who hears say, 'Come.' And let the one who is thirsty come; let the one who wishes take the water of life without cost" (Rev. 22:17). This loving invitation is part of the Bible's final message. It is found five verses from the end. There are no accidents with God. He is the sovereign almighty One, and every word of His Book is in proper order, perfectly composed and clear of message. The everlasting God chose to speak through his servant John, extending the invitation as He closed His written revelation to the human race.

We should make every effort to see that people not only hear about Christ, but that they receive Him as Savior and Lord. Christ invited people, Paul fought to win people, Peter pressed for decisions, and John extended the invitation. Scripture commands that we win people to Christ.

11

Make Disciples, Not Converts

Christ's charge is for us to make disciples, not converts. Breaking out of the holy huddle is not just a concept of finally reaching someone with the Gospel. It also involves training disciples.

The first goal is to help the new believer become a child who delights Father. Then we should help in daily appropriation of the joy which comes with life in all of its fullness (John 10:9-10).

Christ's life was characterized by continually sharing Himself with His disciples. In Mark's report of Christ's appointment of the Twelve, he gives the first purpose, ". . . that they might be with Him" (Mark 3:14). Then they were to go out and preach, having great authority. Biblical evangelism includes helping a child of God learn how to walk with Christ.

Paul stressed discipleship in his uniquely logical way: "And the things which you have heard from me in the presence of many witnesses, these entrust to faithful men, who will be able to teach others also" (II Tim. 2:2). The Biblical norm, therefore, goes far beyond the first generation. We must train faithful disciples so they will be able to train others also.

Give Immediate Attention

It is imperative that we give immediate attention to the new believer. In most cases there is a marked difference between the Christian who receives immediate attention and the one who, after trusting Christ, is left to wander alone. It is my privilege to have a continuing fellowship with a man who came to Christ a relatively short time ago. He has grown and is now actively leading people to Christ and helping others walk with their Lord.

By contrast I remember another Christian from the early days of my Christian experience. Having known Christ less than a year, at nineteen I fervently began to witness to my family members. One of these I unknowingly witnessed to was a relative who was already a Christian. When I witnessed to him I learned he genuinely knew Christ, yet had gone for over a third of a century with very little growth. He had not been led deeper into his faith by those who introduced him to it.

It is not uncommon to meet Christians who know no more about the Word of God today than they did ten years ago. This is tragic and yet true. The first few moments of a new Christian's life are vital. The first few days can mean the difference in the direction of that life.

Paul was not ignorant of the enemy's devices, and we should not be. Peter says that Satan aggressively goes about as a roaring lion, seeking whom he may devour (I Peter 5:8). A new believer left to struggle alone is easy prey for the enemy. Discipleship through more mature Christians is an integral part of God's ordained growth method. If we lead an individual to Christ by the grace of God but do not continue to give personal attention, we are disobedient.

Continue to Share Your Life

Paul's statement to the Thessalonians that he desired to share his life reveals how the best discipleship happens. The second missionary journey began as a discipleship effort. Paul initiated the trip by urging Barnabas to visit the brethren in every city where they had proclaimed the Word of the Lord to see how the believers were (Acts 15:36).

Christ continued to share His life with His chosen ones. From the moment He called those two sets of brothers on the shores of Lake Galilee, He made them a continuing part of His life. Do not simply give the new believer literature or point him to a group. Find a way for yourself or for someone else to share a more mature Christian life with the new believer.

Help Him Learn

The new believer needs to learn how to read the Bible and how to pray.

The Word of God is absolutely essential in teaching how to walk with Christ in love (Ps. 27:8; 119:2). The Bible is our primary source of spiritual nourishment (Heb. 5:12-14; I Peter 2:2). It is the light that shows us how to walk in the darkness (Ps. 119:105, 130), the primary vehicle for determining the will of God (Josh. 1:7-9; Ps. 1:1-3; II Tim. 3:16).

The Holy Spirit gives each Christian a gift when he is

saved (I Cor. 12:1-13) and He nurtures and equips each child for service. There are various gifts operating in the body, but it is the Word of God that uniquely equips the believer with a particular gift for full service (II Tim. 3:17).

There are many other good reasons to read the Bible. It provides us with strength (Acts 20:32; Heb. 5:12-13; I Peter 2:1-2; I John 2:14). It teaches us how to witness (II Tim. 2:15). It is our primary offensive weapon of God's armor (Eph. 6:17). Unless we train the new Christian how to use the Word of God, he or she will stumble and be defeated time after time.

Give Balance

It is easy for a new believer to get started in the wrong direction, or not started at all. He can easily become hyperactive without depth in the riches of grace. On the other hand, he can become an excessively introspective Bible student, forever buried in the holy huddle. It is important in our discipling work that we expose the new believer to the broad scope of Scripture and that we help him balance personal fellowship with the Lord with good works and witnessing.

In addition, the new believer should become aware of the importance of prayer, successfully handling temptations, maintaining a sense of joy in the Christian life, maintaining fellowship through confessing known sin, spiritual warfare, stewardship, love, and the assorted truths involved in Christian growth. Many Christ-honoring organizations have biblically sound discipleship materials. The best materials are the ones you choose to use.

Lead Him to Fellowship

We need each other. The new believer should be encouraged to enjoy the benefits and fulfill the responsibilities of his or her place in the body of Christ. The Bible commands us not to forsake our gathering together. This is necessary in order to hold fast our confession of faith and to stimulate each other to love and good works (Heb. 10:23-25). Every child of God should become active in a local fellowship with other believers. There is no substitute for the local church. Remember, however, to be careful not to let the new believer become trapped in the all too prevalent institutionalization which limits individual gifts and outreach.

Participating in the wonderful merits of the body of Christ, the new believer can also learn to mature lovingly through mutual service. Paul told the Ephesians that proper growth in Christ happens when, speaking the truth in love, the whole body matures through that which every part supplies. Mutual support and growth in love is beautiful (Eph. 4:11-16).

Exercise Prudent Caution

Even the apostle Paul realized, when writing from the prison in Rome, that he had not arrived at perfection (Phil. 3:12-14). Even though Paul was one of the mightiest lives for Christ ever known, he recognized the need for daily growth. There is no shortcut to supersainthood. No ecstatic experience, no acquisition of superior knowledge will achieve that sudden leap to a higher plateau.

In making a disciple, we must be careful that the responsibilities given are appropriate to the new believer's stage of growth. On one hand, encourage spiritual growth; yet, on the other hand, exercise caution lest the new believer with much enthusiasm but little seasoning be thrust into a position beyond his or her capabilities. A new convert should not be a leader (I Tim. 3:6).

Encourage Witnessing

Because a new believer should not assume mature responsibilities right away does not mean that he or she should wait to witness. Even the newest child of God has something to say about what Christ means to him or her. Some of the most dynamic witnesses are those who tell of their Savior while in that fresh new love. I know of one case where a hardened criminal trusted Christ and became an evangelist because of the witness of his five-year-old daughter.

One of my most dramatic experiences involved a man who came to Christ in middle age. He faithfully bore witness to his son, who trusted Christ, who, in turn, led his girl friend to Christ. They were married and she later became my secretary. It was delightful to see her grow in her new-found faith. One day she came trembling into my office to let me know that her father-in-law had gone home to be with his Lord. In one part of our New Life work, eleven members of one family became believers within ninety days as a result of a family member's witness which began just a few days after she had come to Christ.

Encourage the new believer to begin letting others know about the Savior right away. It should be done in love, wisely and tactfully, but with a sense of urgency.

My prayer is that this book will help you to lead the ones you love to the Savior. May many come to you one day in the presence of the Lord Jesus Christ and thank you for caring and introducing them to Him. May many have Christ forever because you, controlled by His love, have taken the message to those for whom He died. And may Christ have all the honor.